I0099845

Sex, Gender and Power

in the Public House

Michael A. Smith

Peacock Press

Sex, Gender, Power in the Public House

© 2013 Michael A. Smith

The names of Public Houses featured have been changed to protect their identity.

All rights reserved. No part of this publication may be reproduced, stored in a retrieval system, transmitted in any form or by any means electronic, mechanical, including photocopying, recording or otherwise without prior consent of the copyright holders.

ISBN 978-1-908904-29-4

Published by Peacock Press, 2013
Scout Bottom Farm
Mytholmroyd
Hebden Bridge
HX7 5JS (UK)

Back cover photo: Jade Smith

Design and artwork
D&P Design and Print
Worcestershire

Printed by Lightning Source, UK

Sex,
Gender,
and Power
in the Public House

Michael A. Smith

Contents

Chapter 1
The Enigma of the Public House:

Virtually everyone has been to a pub, men more than women, but by and large it is a universal experience. Yet with debates about alcoholism, health, and with the extensive nature of change in society, one is wondering where drinking habits are going. What is a pub? Who actually goes to them? When do they go? Why are so many pubs left at the edges oftowns and cities hardly surviving? Of all institutions in our contemporary society the public house myriads much of the best, and some ofthe least, acceptable of behaviour.

This book is about the pub and those people who frequent it. It is more than an exercise to analyse social change. It is an attempt to show that the social, legal and political reality can explain within their own terms part of what it is, and what occurs. They cannot explain the interaction between the elements however they occur, and when they come together, an attempt is made to put the pub and its people on the map. This then is also a foray towards the general thesis that is the out working of chaos theory and a pre-renaissance view of knowledge which counts most in explanation.

1. The social importance of the pub

The pub is a strange context, but immediately one looks at it, it becomes clear that it is differentiated. Each pub has a different history internalised in the regulars who use it. Each pub has a different local history, is set in a different place and has an option on the kind oflandlord it has. Each tends to generate its own culture, its own dominate group depending on the time of day, what activity they are engaged in and how quickly they move on or go home.

I started my pub life in the 1970's, being invited by the University of Salford to lecture in Industrial Change. It was a strange life. Flitting in and out of what appeared much like a modified museum and enjoying the students but not much else. Salford was a typical poor end of the Manchester conurbation. It was where the working class ofthe Victorian period lived. The people lived in small terraced houses and scraped together their small terraced lives. It was where I met Walley the Scrap - a dealer who rented a large scrap yard and Ernie Smith, who owned a shop on lower Broughton Road and whose wife made a pot of tea when I went round. There was George the Malt, a crafty Maltese who made a living out of antiques and there was Harry Levine, the man with a lobotomy operation, who dealt in bric-a-brac. And lastly there was the respectable Albert's Yard, a large area surrounded by a brick wall. Albert's Yard was where one sat by a real roaring fire, and talked about life - over a cup oftea.

It was however an unknown world, full of hunger, doubt, poverty and insecurity, where all relationships seemed temporary but immediate, where there had been a conflict between the church and the pub in the Victorian world - and the pub had won handsomely.

It was nevertheless a real world

What intrigued me was what role had the Pubs played, and did play, in contemporary urban society. If! could make particular claims about work and the shape and structure of society, where did the Public House and alcohol fit into the framework? I turned to the research resources ofthe University, and they were considerable, but found a strange lack of research on the Pub. Also what there was very much confused, condemnatory or segmented type of research, wherever one looked was an uncomfortable reminder that somehow the Pub was a persistent nuisance, alcohol was a dangerous drug, the way of life generated was difficult to fit in with an efficient work life. The Pub and alcohol were treated as dependent dangerous variables or usefully best ignored. As Clinard points our 'Despite the obvious importance of the public drinking house and the perennial controversy over it, most publications about it have been historical accounts, popular articles or propaganda .... studies of the public drinking house as a contemporary social institution are extremely limited ... survey of the literature reveals very few published references' (l). Or as Wilders suggests perhaps most academics are abstemiousness and do not visit public houses (2).

In one sense the problem is to look beyond our cultural framework of European thinking, to stop standing on the shoulders of giants (3), and to develop new insights and explore new propositions and gaps in our understanding.

How does one define a Pub?

The first problem was finding a conceptual definition which sorts out the issues and gives a reasonable start. An approach which gives a basic definition is Clinards,' they are known by a variety of names, such as taverns, bars, pubs, bistros, wine houses and beer halls ... for the purposes of definition one might simply say that public drinking houses are those whose business consists mainly of selling beer, wine or other intoxicating liquors' (4). His defmition suggests thus that the Pub uniquely sells alcohol and is both commercial and public - anyone can buy a drink - thus it is different from private clubs and organisations. He also suggests that it is a group drinking context, it is public behaviour in the presence of others; it must have a publican - who dispenses the drink and oversees behaviour; it has a physical structure and set of social norms, people drink at a bar or table and can take part in various activities and facilities.

The problem with this definition is that it leaves one wondering what is missing, for 'it is no more true to say that people go into public houses to drink than it is to say they go into private houses to eat and sleep' (5). People cannot be dissolved by their behaviour nor can the Pub be deduced in what they do. In an earlier study Selley suggested that the pub is a 'shop where commodities are retailed to the public... differs because it is also a place of meeting ... the atmosphere of the public house is genial...there is companionship, refreshment, enjoyment, change, some recreation, warmth and light... the habit of social companionship accounts for the regular use of the public house (6).

There are clearly some useful pointers to what constitutes the variable and fluid nature of the pub. Yet one wants to know more. Who uses it, in terms of class, sex and age categories? Why do they come, are some factors more important than others? What do people do, are some categories of behaviour and activity more important than others. What are the norms governing behaviour and how do they vary? What kind of perspective do those who work 'behind the bar' have? What are the dimensions of work organisation and how do they relate to the publican's family life and leisure? What kinds of constraint operate in terms of the police, the brewers and the local licensing authorities - constraints which may variously shape the range of activities.

When faced with such questions I asked myself whether I had bitten off more than I could chew, certainly there were many reasonable questions but having opened the box I could do not other than go on. More research was coming to light. Sherri Cavan had recently completed her useful work on bar encounters (7). Another angle was to examine the role of the publican in the organisational matrix (8

A third approach was to attempt a more general framework, but if so how would it all fit together? The historical approach by Monkton who related historical-legal differences in types of alcohol sold by different types of premises at different historical periods (9), is one such type. Another links the patterns of usage and functions for the different types of social groups. This third approach is an attempt to relate the growth of drinking houses to social stratification using the growth of towns and cities and the effects of planning laws and licensing regulations. (10)

It would appear that to establish a type, but which is not an ideal type, containing elements of adequacy is important, however at the same time it has to be firmly empirically established containing the elements of the social sciences. To do this may seem like the Indian rope trick., that collapses or the climber does not return, or like finding the end of the rainbow - when it has moved on. Neither is the case but it does mean looking carefully at the data and building a typology which will fit it into middle range analysis - built from the bottom up.

Types of Public Drinking Houses

The first real clue comes in the linkage between types of pubs and the geographical location and client usage patterns of pub members. It is extensive in the historical distinction between Inns, Alehouses and Taverns.

Inns were originally coaching houses providing refreshment and lodging for travellers and therefore tended to be located on trade routes and busy trade intersections. Since travellers tended to be wealthy these developed as useful recreation centres for the well to do, as well as places where business transactions were conducted.

Alehouses on the other hand, were located in the private cottage or farm kitchen or parlour where 'the good wife would serve a good pot of ale' (11). They were laid out very much like 'a private house or ordinary cottage living room' (12), and 'supplied a purely local need, boasting its own circle of customers, its own collection of taproom ways and characters' (13).

Taverns tended to be the category oflarger inn which was located in the town. In the historical literature the concept suggests a cosmopolitan drinking house for a cross section of the peasants and gentry. As Samuel Johnston commented, "There is no private house .. .in which people can enjoy themselves so well as at a capital tavern ... at a tavern there is a general freedom from anxiety. You are sure that you are welcome; and the more noise you make, the more trouble you give, the more things you call for, the more welcome you are ... there is nothing which is contrived by man by which so much happiness is produced, as by a good tavern' (14). At such taverns congregated' peasantry ... robbers, quacks, moutebanks and undesirables of every kind of both sexes" (15)

Whether peasantry and gentry drank together is perhaps doubtful, but they were certainly contained under the same roof and thus the tavern gathered a somewhat cosmopolitan mixture of patrons.

The distinction between the Inn, the Alehouse and the Tavern, in the historical typology, is not only based on their physical location and where their customers in the social scale derived from but, importantly, on what kind of alcoholic beverages they sold. 'Alehouses were confined to the sale and consumption of ale and beer. Wine was sold and consumed in the Tavern ... the Inn or victualling house was primarily for the use of travellers and sold both beer and wine'.

There was thus an early link clearly established between the kinds of alcoholic drink sold, social stratification of users and physical location of the public drinking house.

This is the connection used by Harrison (16), and whilst much that can be said later about the impact of licensing, the growth of urban industrialisation and the development of the brewing industry, the link between geographical location, social function and the 'class of users' is maintained for analysis of the Victorian period.

Another contribution towards the debate about the types of public drinking houses is the exceptional 1938 'Worktown' Mass Observation Study. The research looks at the' sorts of pub' which then existed and which more or less parallels some aspects of the contemporary situation. Again the classification of types of public drinking houses, as in the previous study, draws a close link between the geographical location, the nature of users and the social role of the public house context.

The study explicitly rejects any distinction between types which depend upon the kind of licence held and the differently named types of pub. 'The legal category of the pub cannot be used as a method of functional classification. Age and topographical factors overshadow law and nomenclature'. (17) However the study goes on to develop an empirical typology based on the size of the public house. 'A more realistic form of pub classification is one based on the large town centre type of pub, the ordinary small beer house, and an intermediate type which may be either a large beer house on a main road, or a small full licence ' .

The larger the pub the more likely it was that the public house was of 'high status'. The study also clearly takes the analysis further by relating the size of public house closely to the 'class of rooms , within them. This is the next step on because it takes our route towards answering the typological question on what has happened between the external changes and the internal organisation of the pub. Apart from claiming that the larger the size the more likely it was that the pub was of 'high status' in terms of the quality of furniture, the floor covering and the 'increasing elaboration of decoration both in the quality of materials used and presence of aspidistras' , the Worktown claim was startlingly obvious. The differences between each pub in terms of size, the larger the better, was also reflected in the types of rooms within the pub, thus 'It is perfectly correct to say that the different types of rooms in pubs represent a graded hierarchy of class, or rather social status, as do the three types of pub' . (18)

So what types of room relate to the three types of pub? Before seeking an answer to such a question, it is worth noting that a graduate student Phil and I paid a visit to Worktown and retraced the pubs they visited - it happened to be the town of Bolton. Of the pubs the Worktown team visited three had now gone, one had converted to a predominantly Asian pub, thus seven were left to ask questions of the regulars.

It was like playing pass the parcel, unwrapping a secret parcel with each layer of wrapping revealing something new - from the names of the pubs (indicated by the Worktown team by a capital letter) to the casual chats with those who happened to be in on that night. It also revealed how difficult a balancing act had to be deployed between drinking (the Worktown team drank half a pint per pub, we drank a pint), detailed questioning as a total stranger, and taking down results in written form, (who uses a pen when in a pub?). These difficulties become more obvious when the actual research problems become questions which have to be answered.

The types of pub externally as large, medium and small as a measure of class differences, were thus elaborated so that within the pub the Worktown research discovered the distinction between the lounge, the taproom and the vault. Each category of internal organisation reflected types of leisure behaviour which fitted the external type of public house.

The small pub was primarily characterised by the vault. The main element in this aspect of our unfolding enigma is that it is an all male context and drinking is done standing. 'You do not come to the vault to relax physically' and it is 'nothing like home'. Men come singly and it is a context of behavioural licence, as one man remarked to the Worktown researcher, ' ... you can do almost anything you bloody well like in the vault'.

The intermediate sized pub was one which included a taproom, had drinks at the same price and was of the same simplicity as the vault, but unlike the vault 'it is entirely a sitting room, wooden benches, wooden stools, unpolished wooden tables, spittoons and dominoes. This is more of a club room than a vault. The same people, the same clothes, the same percentage of caps and scarves'. (19)

The third category was the lounge which had padded seats, chairs, a piano, plants, modem decor, pictures on the wall, never stone floored, no games, waitress service and 'you cannot see the bar from the lounge'. In brief, 'the lounge is a large comfortable room on a middle-class level of comfort with servant and service, everyone in smart clothes'. It was also characterised by sitting at tables and there was no sexual division of usage in that both men and women went into the lounge. 'The vault is the place where men are men. In the lounge they are women's men, with collar studs. For that as usual they pay another penny. '

The classic Worktown study is unique and almost relevant to much of contemporary society. It poses a further set of questions relevant to our quest for a typology of the public house. How far do such sections or rooms exist? To what extent is it possible to distinguish differences in attitudes and behaviour of those using different sections of the pub? Are pub size and location key contemporary criteria in distinguishing public drinking houses? In a theory of knowledge sense, what is the relationship of the physical and social elements? To what extent does the patterning of rooms, location of the bar, furniture and general arrangement of the physical environment influence the patterning of their social meaning? ' ... the experts of the specialised social sciences tend to isolate facts to their own convenience ... filtering them away as family sociology, consuption psychology, anthropology or ethnology of contemporary communities ... they ignore such facts as furniture, objects and the world of objects'. (20) The intention here is to recognise the importance of objects and their constituted social meaning. To some extent the typologies already delineated, particularly the Worktown study, do foster such a recognition.

Before turning to a preliminary ideal type, which we can use when examining the contemporary public drinking house, we should examine the extraordinary usage made of such contexts. There exist over 60,000 pubs in England alone. Some 67% of males visit a pub once or more every month, this figure rising to 76% in the 18-24 age group and falling to 24% of all adult females. (21) What these figures reveal in terms of age and sex usage remains to be revealed. However we have had a glimpse at the patterns of usage and interaction that have been portrayed, the attempts by the academics to take apart various elements, and the considerable difficulties that exist in putting together a picture that makes any sense. What has been intended is a clearer picture of a class, age, work and leisure context that hopefully becomes clearer without falling into the various traps along the way. We ought to examine now what makes for this typology which has for so long been ignored or not understood by social scientists.

Social Dimensions of Usage

Four major interdependent social dimensions of usage can be identified:
   I. It transforms the individual into a social being.

   2. It is a focus of entertainment and social activities.

   3. It is the focus of both drinking and eating.

   4. It is a context for work employment of the publican.

Each of these dimensions can be examined separately and they can reveal how much we have moved on from the various poses adopted before, and the various serious attempts at explanation.

1. The pub is a context where friends gather and existing social relationships are affirmed as well as new ones developed. A network of sociability is created and people interact in terms of shared interests. 'It transforms the individual into a socius'. (22) It is a context which cannot really be explained apart from sociability patterns.

'A great deal of leisure behaviour remains barely comprehensible until the people are brought into focus .. to explain the attraction of public houses it is necessary to shift attention away from the alcohol .. towards the people the activity involves'. (23) Over 60% ofthose who visited a public house frequently went mainly for the company, i.e. sociability, in terms of being with people *and renewing relationships and interests, is an essential part of understanding such a context.*

2. A second dimension of social usage is that of recreational activities in terms of games, music, and the pub as a focus of entertainment and various leisure activities. The pub, when viewed historically, reveals itself as a central feature of community life in both rural and urban areas. It has yet to be proved here that current patterns are class based and moulded in terms of popular culture rather than rational recreation, however there is considerable support for the position adopted by Bailey that historically in terms of urban industrialism, 'Working class leisure was for the most part public and gregarious ... its principal everyday setting was that of the public house ... in an age of dislocation the pub remained a centre of warmth, light and sociability for the urban poor'. (24)

Or as Harrison asserts, 'The lack of open space forced the working people to spend their free time in the drink shop and the public house ... the working man who abandoned the drinking place abandoned far more than drink alone. He was isolating himself from a distinct, vigorous earthy culture.' (25)

The contemporary link between class and recreational patterns of various pubs may be easier to assert than to prove. As Wilders points out: 'There is an absence of detailed investigation of the relationship of the pub to sport and games.' However in an analysis of 273 pubs in Lancashire he found that in 85% darts was played, 87% dominoes, 90% had a fruit machine, 68% had a jjukebox, 63% had a television; folk singing, pop groups, disco and cabaret were reported in less than 5% of public houses surveyed. Interestingly enough the survey tends to confirm the typology developed in the Worktown research, namely, a close relationship between size of premises and 'a noticeable concentration of live entertainment, evening meals and accommodation in the larger classes of public houses'. (26) Although the survey found that 18% of pubs reported club meetings, it also discovered that 'the use of pubs for community functions and meetings, size of the premises is irrelevant'. (26)

3. The third social usage is in drinking itself. The brewers have a major interest in the growth and usage of the changes which have occurred. The growth of supermarkets and the sharp decline of off licence sales attached to pubs since 1960, has meant over 50% of retail sales now occur in non-public house outlets. The growth oflager rather than beer, the increasing pressure to target young people and women as the two fastest growth markets are important.

However the extent to which particular drinks are preferred for different purposes at different times by different categories of users, is still a relatively under-researched area. The Worktown study found that 90% of drink sold was mild, and that the 'regulars' average consumption was three pints a night, the majority of pub goers drinking more at weekends than during the week. Health, refreshment and increasing the appetite were the three reasons for drinking beer, accounting for more than 50% of all reasons given. Women, they found in their research, tended to drink Guinness and 'whisky when they could get it'. There was also an important difference between drinkers in their best room and those in the vault. The research reported that the vault users drank 200% more than those in the best room. (27)

It needs to be emphasised here that concern is not with the biophysiological causes and effects of alcohol consumption. The concern is not with alcohol dependency which is a minority question and no attempt is made to link physiological 'causes' such as alcohol consumption with addiction, or to the social divorce (28). It is instructive to note that it is precisely such an approach which excludes concern with the central question here, namely the nature and effects of normative regulation of alcohol consumption in social contexts namely the public house.

There are central questions which are important in the enigma of the public house. What is the time patterning of drinking activity? To what extent may the time framework change with the drinking activity itself? What are the links between other users of the public house and drinking activity? What are the drinking patterns among the different groups in the drinking context. What are the links between drinking, recreation and sociability? What are the links between drinking and work - both within the pub and the general community?

These are questions which will pervade throughout the analysis in this book but certainly without the value premises that have been identified.

4. The fourth component is the pub as paid employment in the work context. The role of the publican, either as contractual to or as independent of the Brewers, is central. None of the usage patterns thus far identified can afford to ignore the role. The role stands in sharp contrast to the leisure of the participants which involves free-time activities, relatively freely chosen for intrinsic purposes. None of the activities thus far identified, sociability, recreational use, and drinking, may be regarded as 'paid employment'. There are clearly 'rewards', sometimes fmancial, associated with the three functions, perhaps in the sense of gambling in relation to games played, in terms of business meetings and fmancial deals being concluded, perhaps in the 'exchange' situation of buying each other drinks. However viewing the public house as a work context, a situation of paid employment, is an important feature, particularly when the publican is linked to the didactic customer-publican interaction with sociability, recreation and drinking usages of the public house context.

The literature on work in the public drinking house is at best ambiguous. The picture of 'the merry, cheery landlord patronised by rustic regulars holding foaming tankards of ale' (29) contrasts sharply with the working side, 'the place where we laboured the full lawful hours of the clock every day of the year' (30) and 'there is the mistaken idea that all the publican has to do is stand behind the bar looking cheerful, treating his friends to drinks, swapping jokes in doubtful taste and generally being the life and soul of the party' . (31)

The routine of socially policing such a context, the tiring nature of the work, and the problems associated with staff fiddling - so much so that, 'We were all too soon to discover painfully and expensively for ourselves that ... staff are not, generally in a state of original innocence ... barmaids always seemed to hold the strategic initiative .. theft was of course almost universal'. (32), contradict the image of the publican's role as one of constant and trouble-free easy work.

The contrast between the rosy image of the publican's role in the work situation, and the empirical harsh social reality, raises important social issues. Where do such general stereotypes originate, what is the pervasiveness of the approach, what are the mechanisms of its perpetuation? In a more particular sense it suggests a dichotomy in the orientation and experience of those who use the pub for sociability, recreation and drinking, and those who work for a living in tenns of employment, in such a context. There are a lot of questions waiting for answers - and the answers become more important as women become an increasing percentage in what has been predominantly a male institution.

Conclusion

The four categories of usage are important in the study undertaken in this book. There are clues to some generalised social science issues however, embedded in both the typologies outlined in this chapter and the work-leisure usage of the public house. There are two concluding observations which it may be helpful to identify at this point.

1. In what ways and to what extent are public drinking houses stratified in terms of their historical development and contemporary usage? How does such stratification relate to the analysis in class terms of the lifestyles and opportunities of pub goers and users?

2. How important is the pub as a centre of male recreation and leisure? How far can changes in public house subculture be related to changes in sex role stereotypes of maleness and femaleness?

These two issues are not separate, certainly it has been argued that ... 'the persistence of certain key elements of working class culture ... central here is the persistence of the sexual division of labour as the mechanism through which production and reproduction are articulated, and the persistence of cultural definitions of sexual identity ... these two elements ... have played a major role in the historical development and creation of working-class culture ... in non-work cultural forms, this sexual structure also organises the pattern of many elements - for instance the worlds of football and drinking'. (33)

And' ... in the post war period .. the breweries have tended to rationalise (i.e. close) or improve their pubs, with the design changes having had important consequences for the patterns and experience of drinking e.g. the substitution oflarge lounges for a series of snugs, public bars and taprooms. Much of this has been done in accordance with an image of a changing clientele identified by the brewery. The new consumer is ... young ... and classless,' becoming a general 'consumer rather than a member (of a local)'. (34)

In view of these comments we need to look at the changing role of the breweries and the link between work and the public house. In terms of the number of people who go to the pub, the enjoyment that drinking with others gives, the entertainment that the pub provides, and the pub as a hard-working context where people offer a service, it needs to be put on the map.

Chapter 1 References

1. Clinard, Marshall, B., 'The Public Drinking House and Society', p270, in Society, Culture and Drinking Patterns (ed) Pitman and Snyder, Wiley and Co., New York, 1962

2. Wilders, M.G., 'Some Prelininary Discussion on the Sociology ofthe Public House', in Sport and Leisure in Contemporary Society, LSA. 1977 (ed) S.R. Parker

3. Glasser B.O. and Strauss A. 'The Discovery of Grounded Theory', pp 10-11

4. Clinard, op cit p271

5. Gollancz, Victor, 'The Pub and the People', Mass Observation, London 1943 pp 19-20

6. Selley, Earnest, 'The English Public House as it is', Longman Green and Co., 1927 p7

7. Caven, Sherri 'Bar Sociability', in 'People in Places; The Sociability of the Family', edited by A. Birenbaum and E. Sagar in Praegar, New York, 1973 pp 143-154.

8. Hyde PJ. unpublished M. Phil thesis, University of Kent 1974

9. Monkton H.A., 'A History of the English Public House', Bodley Head, London, 1969

10. B. Harrison, Very much the approach, 'Drink and the Victorians', Faber and Faber, 1971

11. Gorham M. and Dunnett H.M.G., 'Inside the Pub', The Architectural Press 1950 p20

12. Ibid, p.20

13. Richardson A.E., 'The Old Inns of England' , Batsford, 1934, p34.

14. Idid p3

15. Ibid p3

16. Harrison B. 'Pubs' pp 161-190, in 'The Victorian City: Image and Realities, Vol 1, edited by H.S. Doys and Michael Wold, Routledge 1973

17. Mass Observation, 'The Pub and the People' 1943, p94

18. Ibid p79-80

19. Ibid ppl00-107

20. Lefebvre Henri, 'Everyday Life in the Modem World' , Allen Lane 1971

21. Bradley M. and Fenwick D., 'Public Attitudes to Liquor Licensing Laws in Great Britain', OPCS London, HMSO

22. Moore E.C. 'The Social Value of the Saloon',AJS Vol3,Nol, 1897, p4

23. Roberts K. 'Contemporary Society and the Growth of Leisure', Longman 1978, p32

24. Bailey P., 'Leisure and Class in Victorian England', Routledge and Kegan Paul, 1978 ppl0-11.

25. Harrison B. 'Drink and the Victorians', Faber and Faber 1971 pp48-50

26. Wilders M.G., op cit

27. Mass Observation, op cit, pp30-34

28. As adopted by the Royal College of Psychiatry Report, 'Alcohol and Alcoholism', 1979

29. Monkton H.A., op cit, pop 99

30. Reynolds H., 'Prisoners in the Bar', Phoenix House, London 1958, p6

31. Cooper D., 'The Beverage Report', Routledge and Kegan Paul, London 1970, pl 09

32. Girton T. 'Come Landlord', Hutchinson and Co., 1957, pp134-6

33. Johnson R. 'Three problematics: elements of a theory of working class culture' , p250, in 'Working Class Culture, Studies in History and Theory', ed., 1. Clarke, C. Critcher and R. Johnson, CCCS, University of Birmingham 1979

34. Ibid p245

Chapter 2
Licensing and Alcohol Consumption

The objectives of this second chapter are twofold. Firstly, to examine attempts which have been made, both legal and social, to control the consumption and sale of alcohol, in terms of particular constraints imposed on the pub. Secondly, to probe the historical social usage of the public drinking house - particularly to the undermass of the population, and their recreation patterns and culture, with some emphases on both the sensuality and masculinity fostered by such a context.

It will be evident in such a strategy that an attempt is made to avoid a strict historical or chronological account of the pub. It would involve a history of alcohol, fascinating as it is, our attention would soon become involved with the minority affected by alcohol consumption. A most threatening trap indeed. Neither is this strictly an historical account of alcoholic drinking patterns. Having said this alcohol and drinking patterns are intimately involved but not as a focus. Rather the purpose is to attempt a critical view ofthe framework of constraints which have influenced the nature and usage of a ubiquitous social context, the public drinking house.

Alcohol and Stereotypes

As has been observed the attempts to control the manufacture and consumption of alcohol are universal, 'As a custom the drinking of alcohol has spread to almost all groups of men ever known and has enjoyed a long life in almost every society of which we have knowledge'. (1)

In specific terms, in relation to English society, the controls over the pub as the context for alcoholic consumption have not evolved in a strict linear historical sense, nor as a rational scheme for social change. Rather they have evolved in the sense of different social, political and legal constraints layered one on the other, so that 'particular provisions owe their existence to specific and sometimes remote historical events'. (2)

What follows next is a closer look at such changes and how the pub acquired the kind of image it came to have. Pub life became entangled with the life of the urban poor, so much so that 'there are singing pubs and swinging pubs, but there are also fighting pubs, pubs frequented by crude spirit drinkers, pubs where knives settle arguments ... criminals congregate not in tea shops but in public houses, as do prostitutes, ponees, social outcasts and other people who don't ever appear in the convivial full page Sunday advertisements. Roger and

Mary sipping their pint and lager respectively in the oak beamed parlour of the Rose and Crown would be genuinely shocked by the conditions under which a large barrelage of beer is consumed'. (3)

There are two questions which are best posed at the outset of this chapter therefore. Why did alcohol become such a problem and remain as part of the stereotype which the local authorities, the brewers, and the politicians saw as part of a threat to middle-class society? How much of a conflict was there between drinking and thinking? What were the general restrictions placed on the pub which may have resulted in a shrinkage of alcohol consumption did the pub suffer the minority image of change generalised by those who see themselves as having legal and brewing power? How far removed were Roger and Mary at the Rose and Crown, from the sensuality and masculinity as the sources of class potential - or was something else involved?

The most powerful stereotypes of the bio-social effects of alcohol consumption is found in the Royal College of Psychiatry Report which asserts that 'Alcohol exerts its most significant effects through the central nervous system. It produces a general sedation or depression of neural activity. Thus ... in appropriate settings alcohol can lesson inhibitions and induce a feeling of well being and euphoria. For many, alcohol relieves tension, nervousness and anxiety'. (4)

Kant's formulation is less scientific, the effect of alcohol consumption being, he argued: 'carefreeness, and with it the lack of caution intoxication produces, is a result of an illusionary feeling of increased vitality', and again, 'drunkenness is the unnatural state of inability to organise sense impressions according to the laws of experience'. (5)

The bio-social mode of analysis underpins much of contemporary analysis with the 'problem' and its possible addiction producing qualities. Thus 'alcohol must be considered a drug who's pharmacological action is intermediate in kind and degree between addiction producing and habit forming drugs, so that compulsive craving and dependence can develop in those individuals if their make-up leads them to seek and find an escape in alcohol. With this substance the personal make-up is the determining factor'. (6)

There is no intention here of entering into the debate about the aetiology and nature of alcoholism. What is intriguing is that in such an analysis there is almost no recognition that the context of alcohol consumption and drinking styles of individuals may have an effect on the level consumed. To put the case slightly differently it tends to make personality theory the cause and drinking the effect, rather than the contexts in which alcohol is sold and consumed. It is intriguing that the increased drinking of alcohol outside the pub has virtually paralleled its emergence as a social 'problem'. Non-public house sales now account for more than 50% of all sales, so that 'a revolution in drinking habits is gathering momentum in Britain, mainly as a result of the emergence of the high street supermarket multiple'. (7) The point being made is an important if simple one, namely, that the psychopathology of alcoholism, and individual personality variables as casual elements explaining alcohol consumption patterns, should not be confused with a social context of drinking behaviour. Without an understanding of this point it is easily missed that less than a third of those who go into pubs report that they do so solely for the purpose of drinking (8), and that 'As well as the beer in your glass, the deal includes the barmaid's smile or the landlord's bonhomie, the opportunity to buy a sandwich or have a game of darts, the chance either to fmd a comer to chat with friends, or stand at the bar and meet a stranger to the pub'. (9)

One social stereotype of the pub is that it is closely linked to dangers of alcohol addiction to the individual. Also there is a persistent image ofthe public house as an unruly context, the place where criminals meet each other, where elements of violence and the underworld meet.

The autobiographical experience of one publican is revealing thus: 'At least 60% of our customers, both male and female, have been guests of H.M. Government at various times ... the men have spent a proportion of their time in jail for almost every conceivable kind of petty thieving and trickery from nonexistent Xmas turkeys to some fairly large warehouse break-ins ... we became fairly knowledgeable about the amenities of different prisons'. (10) The social stereotype of the public drinking house being linked to criminality; moral deviance and the nurturing of a Bacchanalian pleasure ethic rather than social respectability and a rational civilising morality is drawn by one early nineteenth century writer, thus: 'In Manchester alone there are very near if not quite 1,000 inns, beer houses and gin-vaults ... ministering their poisons to thousands of debilitated creatures ... nor is it the adult male labourer who alone visits these receptacles for everything that is wicked and degrading ... all ages come here, herding promiscuously with prostitutes, pick pockets, and various scum and refuse of society, all jumbled up together in a heterogeneous mass of evil'. (11)

Thus far two stereotypes have been identified which underpin the impetus for social control over the sale and consumption of alcohol and the usage of the public house; firstly the potential deleterious effects on the individual and thus of wider society of unrestrained alcohol, and secondly the threat that a widespread existence of the pub might pose by fostering a 'subversive culture' in opposition to a rational social order. It is interesting to know if it is incidental that these two stereotypes are influenced by a third force, that which claims that work as rationality is the supreme moral and economic virtue as the pivot of a work -centred and organised society, a society in which technology-based production and management thinking increasingly replace the pub as a measure of the civilising morality, where the 'torpor of the faculties' and the morality of self indulgence are replaced by the microchip efficiency and legalised formal contractual relationships. The claims of Samuel Smiles illustrate vividly the values deriving from the morality of work as a supreme ethical principal. As he said 'Work is one of the best educators of practical character. It promotes and disciplines obedience, self control, attention, application and perseverance ... work is the law of our being - the living principle that carries man and nations forward ... true happiness is never found in the torpor ofthe faculties but in their action and useful employment'. (12)

The development of an 'ideology of work' (13) and the necessity of a socially 'healthy' population, it is suggested, underpin the social stereotypes of alcohol consumption, particularly in terms of social controls, in two particular forms. Firstly in terms of the legal controls imposed on alcohol consumption in relation to the public drinking house. Secondly in constraints on recreational and voluntary activities which have formed the core of a play dimension of the public drinking house. These two aspects constitute the focuses in the following two sections of this chapter.

Licensing and Legal Controls

Licensing, a regulation of the manufacture and sale of alcohol, 'Originated not in any abstract theory but in a practical necessity of the state. It was found that the free use of intoxicating drink produced not only incapacity and disease among all classes, but also, among the lower orders, idleness and disorderly living, crime against life and property and even riot and rebellion'. (13)

The social control objective of legal licensing is thus, according to the Webbs, fairly unambiguous. Thus 'For more than three hundred years the manufacture and sale of alcohol has been brought under special statutory regulation ...

The primary objective of this legislation has been to prevent social disorder and personal misconduct brought about by excessive drinking (14)

Since the manufacture of alcoholic beverages in their various forms was a 'home industry', control developed over the sale of such beverages rather than any attempt to regulate their manufacture. Licensing policy therefore has been concerned with controlling who has the right to sell alcohol and under what conditions. Two elements however have complicated the situation; the early realisation that tax could be levied and raised by a duty on alcoholic drinks, and the political influence of Brewers and the economic importance of the brewing industry. The levying of taxes has always been an issue for national government, whilst local government has been primarily responsible for the sale of alcoholic drinks and the conditions under which they are consumed. As the Webbs point out the function oflicensing, delegated by Parliament to the local Justices of the Peace, has always included three distinct forms ofthe control:

1. The power of selection - which persons (and later premises) shall be designated as licensable for the purpose of selling alcoholic drinks.

2. The power of withdrawal - statutory formal registration and selection also entails the right to withdraw approval - to prohibit particular persons (and later particular premises).

3. The power to impose conditions - this power was not conferred by statute until after 1830, but prior to that time evolved naturally from the powers of selection and withdrawal. (15)

The history of licensing legislation is a long and complex one, and it is doubtful if any particular analytical purpose is served by a recitation of individual statutes and acts - even if one could disappear down this white rabbit hole and eat things which make one much bigger - no, the intention is to examine the general licensing prior to the 1830 Beer House Act. Then to examine since that time the particular features of legislation and legal controls which govern both sale and consumption of alcoholic drinks. It is the latter which penetrates the historical and contemporary leisure dimensions and usage patterns of the public drinking house.

The general assessment is subject to four particular kinds of influence. Firstly, local licensing justices had wide-ranging discretion, thus there is seldom a homogeneous set of effects deriving from a particular piece of legislation. Secondly there were after 1830 major changes occurring in the structure of the brewing industry, changes which were to lead to the 'tied house' system and monopolistic trends in manufacture, particularly the manufacture of beer. Thirdly, powerful social movements, such as the movement for Free Trade or the movement for Temperance, and particular events - such as war - have exerted their influence on the economic, political and social arena. Fourthly, the historical sources tend to be written by the literate and articulate - often how a particular layer of society perceived and experienced change, and may tell us little about the poor and illiterate. It was the poor and illiterate however who formed the bulk of the population, who were most affected by legislation increasing control required for mechanised work and factory routines. These four limiting factors are dealt with variously in this chapter, and the next, and thread their way through some of the debated issues posed by the history and social usage of the public drinking house.

As early as 1552, in the first licensing by statute, local Justices of the Peace were authorised to 'select certain persons to each county or borough who were to exercise the trade of keeping an alehouse' . (16) By 1729 the Brewster sessions were instituted which regularised the granting of licences and effectively bestowed on Justices the power to create licensed premises, favour certain interests, and impose conditions in relation to the sale of ale. The introduction of Brewster Sessions resulted from a particular situation.

The first was the increasing nepotism of individual Justices deciding applications in isolation, without public scrutiny. The second was the effect of war with France, there was a shortage of French brandy resulting from import prohibition after 1690. This prohibition between 1690 to 1729 lead to 'a perfect pandemonium of drunkenness ... not only were there in London and Westminster six or seven thousand regular gin dram shops, but cheap gin was given by masters to their work people instead of wages, sold by barbers and tobacconists, hawked about the streets on barrows by men and women '.' vended by pedlars in suburban lanes, and freely offered in every house of ill fame'. (17) The situation between 1690 and 1729 could not be tolerated whereby 'general permission was granted to all persons to distil and retail English spirits profligency in terms of dram (gin) shops and ale houses. By 1722 it has been estimated that 36 gallons of ale were consumed for every man, women and child in the population. (19) The establishment of the Brewster Sessions in 1729 coincided with the requirement of licensing of dram shops and in 1736 the sale of all spirits was restricted to publicans licensed by the local Justices

By the Act of 1753 licence applicants had to support their application with a statement of personal character, which meant obtaining a personal testament from a clergyman and church warden or several householders. This provided the Justices with an additional restrictive weapon, and even a 'public vestry' control mechanism. 'From the standpoint of the present day the most notable action taken ... was the suppression up and down the country of public houses, without compensation, sometimes because they were complained of as disorderly, as ill-constructed, or as improperly situated, but frequently because they were deemed superfluous - affording injurious encouragement to the consumption of intoxicating drinks'. (21)

In 1787 the Sheffield Justices closed all dram shops in town whilst two years before, in 1785, the St. James Westminster Justices decided that 'constables and beadles do return lists of the names victuallers and any other persons who shall set up or keep a bawdy house, or house of ill fame, or shall permit, suffer or set up any billiard or other gaming, or any shuffle board or suffer any skittle playing'. (22) The Justices went further threatening to proceed against any publican who 'shall keep his or her house open in the night or suffer any drunkenness or tippling, or any dancing or music ... no licence be afterward granted to the house where the offence was committed'. (23)

The Webbs' estimate that by 1773 there were not less than 100,000 licensed houses for a total population ofless than 8 million people. By 1825 the number of spirit licences was 38,472 and ale houses approximately 40,000.

The situation prior to 1830 therefore was that legally the consumption and sale of alcohol was constrained. Justices were generally refusing new licences, withdrawing licences from houses of ill repute, and closing down establishments where there were considered too many in any particular area. Interestingly the Webbs suggest that such changes were reinforced by the growth of a number of important factors, 'A new Evangelical zeal for saving men's souls, a growing dislike by the propertied classes of the insecurity of life and property, the alarm of the financier and the ratepayer at the increasing burden of the poor rate, and last but not least, the half conscious desire of the rising class of industrial capitalists to drive the manual worker out of the ale house and gin shop into the factory and workshop'. (24)

It is obvious perhaps that the Free Trade movement and the Temperance movement to a large degree conflicted, the latter being concerned with absenteeism and a commitment to life which demanded duty, obedience and family, whilst the former extolled trade freedom internally and emphasised all that went with such freedoms. There are however two consequences which directly result from licensing legislation and increased Justices control over the drinking premises. Firstly the shift by brewers towards tied outlets whereby the pub was bought by the brewer - the capital costs and good public tenant ensured this. Secondly registration that the pub was the place which appealed to the 'lower orders' and this was a style of life which was at variance with rational time-structured routines. Thus in the 1830's 'Working-class leisure was for the most part public and gregarious and [that] its principal for everyday setting was that of the public house .. the institutional hub of working class recreation'. (25)

In 1828 a new Ale House Act consolidated all previous licensing legislation and defined the jurisdiction of licensing Justices for the next hundred years. The granting of a full publican's licence was recognised as the only one which authorised the publican to retail any kind of alcoholic beverage. Brewster Sessions were regularised at a minimum of four and a maximum of eight per year. Licences could be renewed or transferred at such sessions. The licensee did not have to provide good character references and accepted certain conditions, which failure to keep would result in legal penalties. Finally the conditions which had to be accepted by a publican in keeping a good house were as follows; not to adulterate the alcoholic beverages sold, to use only legal and properly stamped measures, not to permit drunkenness, unlawful games or the gathering of 'bad characters' on the premises, and not to open during Divine service on Sundays, Christmas or Good Friday. (26)

At the same time as the Act licensing the Ale House came into being, the Free Trade movement gained momentum and in 1830 introduced the Wellington Beer House Act. Any person whose name was on a rate book might open his premises as a beer shop free from any Justice's licence or control, simply by payment of two guineas to the local office of excise. The effects were dramatic, largely reversing the previous fifty years of strict and harsh control, and within six months, some 24,342 new beer sellers had come into being and by 1838 the number was 45,717. The effects were such that 'everyone is drunk. Those who are not singing are sprawling. The sovereign people are in a beastly state'. (27) As the Webbs point out 'Not only was beer now sold at every bakers and petty chandlers shop; regular drinking places were opened in cellars and back premises in every alley in town slums ... it is easy to imagine in the absence of any efficient police, accompaniments of gambling, brutal amusements and licentiousness, which the competition of beer-sellers for custom encouraged'. (28) One of the main objectives of the 1830 Wellington Beer House Act was to reduce consumption of gin and encourage the sale of 'healthy' beer. The initial effect was the reduction of gin sales, but this reduction turned to a 15% - 20% increase as indicated by the 1857 first of the Commissioners of the Inland Revenue. The new beer houses continued unrestrained, even in 1834 the House of Commons Committee on Drunkenness, new Beer House Act meant that there was 'not once such place to every twenty families throughout the United Kingdom'. The rising middle class in the 1830's was immediate and hostile, 'the first results of the Free Trade in beer had caused a perfect panic among those responsible for peace and law and order ... the winter had in the south of England been one of almost constant uproar and sullen rebellion, during which ricks had been burned and machinery destroyed ... petitions from Justices, clergymen, churchwardens and overseers, vividly described the horrors ... the tippling, the late hours, the noise, the disorder, the gambling, the receiving of stolen goods or proceeds of poaching, the filling of prisons and the raising of the poor rate'. (29) The regulation of beer houses was left to the constabulary but was also subject to growing pressures from the rising middle classes. The pressure also came from existing publicans with a full licence who suddenly became aware of the threat posed by the unlicensed houses, 'Publicans made shift to outpace their rivals ... hence the gin palaces and the regular entertainment of the singing saloon'. (30) The pressure to contain beer houses gave impetus to the establishment in the early 1840's of working men's clubs or 'moral beer houses ... a simple retreat, furnishing warmth and light, bread and cheese, baccy and beer .. .' and interestingly these were gradually supported by middle-class reformers with an acceptance that such clubs would 'foster moderation by moving men out of the range of the publican with his encouragement of traditional customs such as treating and tossing'. (31) As already suggested the newly formed constabulary took some action and in the 1839 Police Act, public houses in the metropolis of London were required to close from midnight on Saturday to 1 pm on Sunday. By 1848 all public houses in England were closed on a similar basis. However public houses remained open all the time (apart from the Saturday night to Sunday morning time slot) until the first World War in 1914.

The whole situation was integrated in the Wine and Beer House Act with the beer houses being brought firmly under jurisdiction oflocallicensingjustices. Existing holders of the two guinea licence could not be refused a new licence except on one of four grounds: failure to show good conduct; keeping of a house of bad character - thieves or prostitutes were such 'bad characters'; previous disqualification on the grounds of misconduct; and finally a situation where the applicant or house were not 'duly qualified by law'. (32) The 1872 Licensing Act tightened the licensing regulations for all retail sales of alcoholic beverages, including the sale of spirits to those under sixteen years of age, the right of Justices to transfer licences within and between districts, the introduction of 'early closing licences', and increased penalties for adulteration of beverages and contravention of the licensing laws. (33)

The pressure to legislate to curb the open provision for the sale of alcoholic beverages continued in the late nineteenth century particularly with temperance reformers and those who saw change as possible in the working-class education movement. Reinforcing both were the trends in rational recreation which was 'An attempt to forge more effective behavioural constraints in leisure ...' by introducing working men to 'the satisfactions of mental recreation, thus immunising them against the contagion of the pub and the publican, and the animal regression of sensuality', however 'despite the legislative curtailment and the loss of some of its functions to more specialised institutions, the pub continued to offer the irreducible attractions of drink and good fellowship'. The situation by the 1880's, suggests Bailey, shows one of considerable change from fifty years previously, so much so that 'with certain gross exceptions drink was becoming more of an incidental social lubricant and less of a total experience'. (34)

The twentieth century has seen the dominance of the brewers and the Justices which have constrained the sale and consumption of alcohol, although in the context of this book, this containment contains certain assumptions which suggest that the pub is not dead, just sleeping. This suggests that alcohol consumed outside the pub as a drinking context, the rise of feminism, the growth of ethnic minorities, the retention of a class-based distribution system of pubs, and the recent freeing of pub opening hours, poses new tensions in the relationship. Thus the piece of legislation which followed is the Licensing Planning Act of 1945 which resulted from the Morris Committee findings on War Damaged Licensed Premises. The committee wanted in short to see new patterns of drinking, improved contexts and a fairly radical resitting policy. Thus 'the replacement ... of two or more small licensed houses by one larger one in order to provide a unit of better size, and the distribution of these amalgamated units more rationally', and provide 'in appropriate cases the enlargement of the site of the premises to provide outdoor amenities, such as gardens or bowling greens', inside the public house 'to provide more comfort and space per customer and to enable seats and tables to be more fully available', and fmally the Act allowed for 'the provision of ... light refreshments or snacks with the service of drink in the bars, and of non-intoxicating drinks'.

The effect of the Act was to give approval by local licensing authorities to create single large public houses, and the Licensing Planning Committee in the thirty two large areas of population (including London, Manchester, Birmingham and Sheffield). The effect has been largely as intended that in the post-war era we have seen large new 'dry' suburbs, the creation of 'large units' and the fostering of 'new drinking styles'. The effect in terms of 'need' was to define the new public drinking house as meeting the requirement of one public house to every thirty thousand of the population. Consequently in some areas no new pubs were built since 'need' was sufficiently met by existing pub provision, in other areas the criteria meant that no new pubs were envisaged until after the population level had reached the appropriate criteria. One of the effects of this has been that often 'the local' is only available by car - with the effects this has on 'drinking and driving'.

Perhaps it is to adopt too conspiratorial a view to suggest that all licensing legislation derives from the historical growth of a rising middle class and a civilising morality, both of which conflicted directly with pre-industrial values and customs and the emergence of a working-class culture within industrialism. However this seems very much to echo the works by Bailey (35) and Harrison (36) as suggested by Marcuse, namely 'The rising middle class based their demand for a new social freedom on the universality of human reason. But freedom and reason did not extend beyond this group's interest - to accusing questions the bourgeoisie gave an affirmative answer, affirmative culture ... to the needs of the isolated individual it responds with general humanity, to bodily misery with beauty of the soul, to external bondage with internal freedom, to brutal egoism with the duty of the realm of virtue .... ' (37)

There is little doubt that the twentieth century has witnessed the decline of absolute alcohol consumption. Importantly has it changed also that 'hub of working-class recreation and sociability', the multiple activities and interests which the public house fostered? The focus is from the 1830's onwards, and very much as before, there are a number of specific reasons for this; new urban dwellers were not far removed from the land, and the leisure and work routines of pre-industrial culture are still important; there was growing importance of the constabulary; the period witnessed the growing influence of the middle classes in an attempt to establish rational recreation. Also the temperance movement was only beginning to develop in the 1830's and the full extravagance of nineteenth-century drinking houses had yet to grace the urban scene.

The Pubs Social Arena

The public drinking house, as indicated in chapter one, was divided between inns, taverns and alehouses, each having its set of regulars, the alcohol it sold, the recreational activities it encouraged, and the links it had with its community. However the eighteenth century saw these three types gradually come together so that by the 1780's the inn and the tavern were virtually the same in terms of the drinks available and recreation offered; the alehouse was still separate but with Izack Walton's romantic famous saying about the alehouse in the Compleat Angler, whereby' I am glad that your patience hath held out for so long for we are now in sight of the thatched house. I'll now lead you to an honest Alehouse, where we shall find cleanly rooms, lavender in the windows and twenty mallards stuck about the wall. There my hostess, which I may tell you is both cleanly handsome and civil, hath dressed many a fish for me.' (38), soon was to pass as a rural image and lead to the mug of ale as 'the primordial cell of British social life' . (39)

The alehouse however was closely linked to the customs and traditions of a rural culture - a culture in which animalistic and traditional orgiastic celebration were closely woven into a strong behavioural and oral tradition. The public house when finally it emerged in the early nineteenth century carried this culture forward and this is why the new gin palaces and beer houses were so out of place with strict middle-class demands of work and the social norms governing social life.

The sort of sweet shop full of lollipops, so much so that I want it and I want it now, must have clashed with the demands of mine owners, mill owners and methodists, the growth of new mills, new factories, and the large urban poor were basically incompatible. Perhaps what has been so graphically depicted by Hogarth with gin drinking linked to debauchery and poverty, as contrasted with beer drinking linked with respectability and the empty pawnbrokers' shop, industry and idleness constituted an attempted change of some moment.

It was the flamboyant gin palace which emerged in the early nineteenth century, along with the threat of the new unlicensed beer houses in the 1830's, so much so that 'In the 1830's the publican had every reason for enriching shop fa~ades which had gripped London in the 1820's, for the Beer House Act of 1830 had created a new rival for his custom. A new phenomenon, the gin palace - with plate glass windows, richly ornamental fa~ade, gilded lettering and brilliant lamps - began to arouse comment. Its style became almost uniform in urban pubs. Its splendour accentuated the contrast between the pub and the squalor of its surroundings ... the predominance of the nineteenthcentury gin palace' illustrates the theory that' .. .it was specially designed for the casual urban drinker. Whereas the pub had originally been nothing more than an enlarged home, city life demanded a large shop with specialised equipment .. a long bar, enclosing several assistants, easy access to large quantities of alcoholic drink, racked in attractively painted casks on the back wall; a large area before the bar where many customers could move freely ... '. (39)

Or as Bailey observes 'The new pubs built in the 1830's - the so called gin palaces - were entirely different in scale, in layout, in style and management. They solved the problem of space by doing away with seats, they also discouraged dawdling, which in tum meant a more rapid turnover in customers. Any feeling of congestion among the new generation of perpendicular drinkers was relieved by the upward spaciousness provided by higher ceilings and the illusion of roominess contrived by the use of mirrors and plate glass. The huge gas lamps ... hung outside as well as inside, and extended the territory of the pub into street at all hours of the night. A bar counter separated the customer from the liquor and its customers, indicative of a more business-like approach ... the domesticity of the old pub had given way to the commercialised glamour of new people's palaces, gaudy compensation for the meanness of everyday life'. (40)

The emergence of the gin palace was stimulated by the fifth category which was born out of the 1830 Beer House Act. The explosion of beer houses shared little else except they were frequented by the new urban poor, were small and relatively uncommercialised and extremely numerous, and fostered the styles of life and drinking habits in the context of social life for a largely illiterate and unsanitised mass.

The beer house along with the more flamboyant gin palace, entrenched the social usage of the earlier alehouse with the rural cultural traditions, traditions which included animalism and orgiastic celebration, a sense of sensuality and masculinity although in a much more stratified form, gave birth to the contemporary pub, thus' .. .in an age of social dislocation the pub ... was a centre of warmth, light and sociability for the urban poor, a haven from the filth and meanness of inadequate and congested housing, a magnet for the disoriented newcomer and disgruntled regular alike'. (41) Such meanness of housing and disorientation were not helped by the lack of purified water as a system and the pub as offering the safe 'mug of ale'. The following figures show both the ubiquity of the public house and the rate of decline of the licensed institution:

Year	Total Licences	Persons Per On-Licence
1831	82,484	168
1841	91,612	174
1851	95,484	188
1861	107,696	186
1871	112,884	201
1881	106,910	243
1891	105,006	276
1901	102,841	316
1911	90,586	398
1921	82,411	458
1931	77,049	517
1941	73,210	571
1951	73,421	595

Such a decline in the licensed institution (42) reveal not only the decline of the public house as such, but interestingly the explosive increase in the population during such a period.

People found the tyranny of Victorian capitalism and exploitative labour in a vicarious immediacy and existential experience, not altogether uninformed by the growth of rational recreation, in the public drinking house. Such a claim requires substantive proof and the evidence, which is complex, scattered and subject to various interpretations - not least by historians, continues to exist. It is clear that the public house is a diverse, variable and changing context, the social characteristics of which may differ in scope, pervasiveness and stability over time. In general however the view is taken from the bottom up, and this is the way through to some meaningful interpretations of what has happened to the pub. In general however, it is claimed here that the context is an extension of the social values, sociability patterns and role networks of its participants. What can be asserted here, with some confidence however, is that the pub in the nineteenth century was patronised by the new mass of urban dwellers, that such dwellers were usually poor and working class, and that the public house became geographically located and socially anchored in a variety of garish, splendid and diverse contexts characteristics of the period.

The key to understanding the diversity of public house life is to focus on the patterning of usage. Some have claimed that 'Statistics cannot tell what these pubs were doing'. (43) Perhaps the full account of the social nature of pub life cannot be written, interwoven as it has been with street life, slum subculture, the transformation of Alehouse oral and sensual traditions, the development of new work routines both inside and outside the pub, and the diverse places which provide for a kaleidoscope of human interaction. There is no particular concern to develop an ideographical historical approach, the concern is to explore three primacies of the social usage patterning as the conclusion to this chapter on what for many is still a central institution of the twenty ftrst century. Firstly as a focus of community life and criminal subculture, secondly as the dominant mode of working-class usage, and thirdly as a centre for recreation, entertainment and sexual licence. The relationship between the pub and these three areas still starts in the I830s. The relationship with work merits separate attention and is dealt with in chapter three.

The inter-meshing between the pub and street and community life was a considerable part of Victorian existence, for 'many people earned their living on the pavement - the beggars, stall holders, acrobats, organ grinders, peddlers, whom Mayhew interviewed so brilliantly', for the barrier between the pub and the street was easily crossed for 'the two worlds were connected by great areas of glass, by first-floor balconies, by pavement seats and tables, by potmen carrying cans of ale in wooden frames to customers in nearby premises, and by a multitude of entrances', some pubs having three such entrances, and exits. (44) The absence of open space in the period was a reinforcing element in the social life of the street therefore 'As footpaths, public gardens and common land were swallowed up or subjected to property rights, the street alone was left as the new commons of the industrial poor enlivened by the diversion and entertainment of its many professional habituees; Punch and Judy men, buskers, ballard hawkers, street preachers, stump orators and patent medicine salesmen. The street was also an informal meeting place for gossiping neighbours as a seasonal promenade for the young and flirtatious .. .it was not just the problem of open space but of adequate indoor facilities as well; moreover there was the increasing pressure of sheer numbers .. the pub was the natural resting place for the increase in human traffic'. (45) It was thus with the importance of the gregariousness and community of street life that the pub began to assume its new significance.

This side of public house advancement also had a criminal side to its activities, given the link between vice, prostitution and the fostering of not only idleness amongst the urban poor, but crimality and a vicious threatening underworld, so much so, 'where hundreds of thousands grew up in undrained, unpoliced, undergoverned and underschooled urban poor', and where 'pauperism, filth, overcrowding and crime were intimately connected', where 'low public houses were often the scenes of all sorts of brutality' . (46) The streets themselves and the housing conditions in which the poor lived were not jolly picturesque places, 'the houses are ill drained, often ill ventilated, unprovided with privys and in consequence, the streets which are unpaved, narrow and worn into deep ruts, become the common receptacle of mud, refuse and disgusting ordure ... near the centre of the town [Manchester] a mass of buildings inhabited by prostitutes and thieves, is ... intercepted by narrow and loathsome streets ... there is only one privy for 380 inhabitants ... cess pools with open grids .. gullies, down which filthy streams percolate; and the inhabitants are crowded in dilapidated abodes or obscure and damp cellars'. (47) The public house was without doubt a heaven of warmth, light and sociability, compared to the often polluted streets and netherskens, this latter containing 'a shifting collection of casual labourers, hawkers, beggars thieves, one-night stand prostitutes, petty tarts and sharpers, road sweepers, street performers, broken servants and other more or less unspecified riffraff', and making the link between such conditions and criminality, the publican and the pub, 'thousands of our felons are trained from their infancy in the bosom of crime ... familiarised with vice from their earliest years ... carried to the beer shop or gin palace on the breast of worthless drunken mothers'. It was the 'licenced victuallers who had close connection with lodging house keeping' and were 'scandalously influential on watch committees' , and 'in the tap room of flash pubs .. was carried on the essential traffic of the underworld. Here robberies wefe hatched, disposal of stolen property arranged .. above all information bought and exchanged .. what could be better than a public house, open from dawn to midnight, where no visitor's presence need mean anything more than a wish for a drink? Except for modern gin palaces, pubs in working-class districts usually carried on their trade in pokey little apartments that lent themselves to confidential meetings. Pubs in towns were often on corner sites with entrances (and exits) on different streets. Often too, thefe was a high gated yard where a trap could be loaded Of unloaded in comparative privacy'. In short pubs often lay at the heart of the criminal underworld. (48) The 'condition of England ' problem resulted in improvements in housing and living conditions, in rigorous local authority planning controls, in improvements in public health, in growing police powers, and then with new patterns of recreation and consumerism, yet has it changed this basic criminal subculture of pub, its convenience and ease, its secretive nature? It may have declined, but by how much, is a matter for empirical research. What is clear however is that in some important aspects the pub was colonised as an ideal context for criminal subculture with strong linkages to prostitution and various forms of illegal activity, a nexus to the criminal underworld.

The Dominance of Working-Class Usage

It often has been assumed that in general 'we are all middle class now', but this may not be the case however, especially when the pub is looked at in detail. In fact the opposite may be nearer to the truth, that the wOfking class have been prepared to 'take in' the middle class therefore 'we are all working class' if one takes the fecent self definition into account. Thefe is without doubt a containment of working-class activities surrounding the pub, but how far this amounts to a middle-class patterning of the sensual and masculine pub usage patterns depends again upon the findings of empirical research. It also depends significantly upon the changing nature of femaleness in a pub situation.

How did that dominance of a 'working -class' context come about, what were the factors influencing the reinforcement in the 1830 onwards? Precisely where the drinking contexts were located in major population centres itself affords a clue. They were more popular in city centres than in the leafy suburbs, and more likely that in terms of working-class housing, one would find them 'strategically placed .. providing the working man with his journey to work and with refreshment on his way home'. (49) It can be speculated that the period of 1830 to 1869 provided the basis for this patterning, with consolidation of pub geography taking place from 1870 to 1945, with major restrictions (thus leafy and not too leafy suburbs) where after 1945 new suburbs came into being. The population increased from under 8 million in 1801 to over 34 million in 190 I which suggests the breweries followed where most people lived, whose everyday world was the streets, the netherskens, the factory and the sweat shops. In such a situation leisure was time and spatially constrained. By the late 1860's the average working week was still seventy hours and included the Saturday. The immediate playground was the urban industrial scene where the pubs and chapels were the two dominant features 'the former were seldom closed and the latter seldom open'. (50) The conflict between the ideals, values and life-styles fostered by the pub and those encouraged by the chapel was real. The attack was on the inefficiency induced by working class life centred around the public drinking house. 'The English workingclass may be said to be soaked in beer. They are made dull and sodden by it. Their efficiency is sadly impaired and they lose whatever imagination, invention and quickness might be theirs .. the public house is ubiquitous. It flourishes on every street corner and between corners .. as home life vanishes, the public house appears. Not only do men and women abnormally crave drink, who are overworked, exhausted, suffering deranged stomachs and bad sanitation, and deadened by the ugliness and monotony of existence, but the gregarious men and women who have no home life flee to the bright and clattering public house .. wretchedness squirms for alleviation, and in the public house its pain is eased and forgetfulness is obtained. It is unhealthy. Certainly it is, but everything about their lives is unhealthy, while this brings the oblivion that nothing in their lives can bring'. (51)

We have to make carefully the suggestion of the public house in terms of its dominance of working-class life and sociability. We have to be aware of possible distortions in historical evidence, the evidence itself showing that the inarticulate, by definition, leave few records of their thoughts .. it is easy to make a false division into the organised and chapel-going good, and the dissolute bad, in the industrial revolution, since the sources push us in that conclusion ... 'Firstly the facts that 'in 1800 there were fifty thousand harlots, five thousand publicans and ten thousand thieves in London alone', and that 'impressionistic estimates ... reveal as much about the mentality of the propertied class as they do about the criminal behaviour of the un-propertied .. taverns, fairs, and any large congregation of people [were regarded as] a nuisance - sources of idleness, brawls, sedition or contagion'. Thus the sources tend to reflect the 'Utilitarian attitude of the new manufacturing class, whose need to impose a work discipline in the factory towns made it hostile to many traditional amusements and levities.' Thirdly there was the influence of Protestantism, particularly, 'Methodism itself, with its unending procession of breast beating sinners, popular confessional biographies from the press ... such must be held up to Satanic light and read backwards'. Finally it is suggested that 'when we come to assess the early working class movement.. some of the first leaders and chroniclers were self-educated working men, who raised themselves by efforts of self discipline which required them to turn their back on the happy go lucky tavern world ... those who have wished to emphasise the sober constitutional ancestry of the working-class movement have sometimes minimised its more robust and rowdy features'.

We need to take such claims carefully and the reason is clear since 'we need more studies of the social attitudes of criminals, of soldiers and sailors, of tavern life; and we should look at the evidence not with a moralising eye, but with an eye for Brechtian values - the fatalism, the irony in the face of establishment homilies, the tenacity of self preservation ... the inarticulate conserve certain values - a spontaneity and capacity for enjoyment and mutual loyalties - despite inhibiting pressures of magistrated, mill owners and methodists'. (52)

Some care has been taken thus far to avoid an ideographical historical approach or an ethical stance in relation to the nature and usage of the public drinking house. What has been suggested is that this has been closely integrated with working-class culture and lifestyles, this is not to suggest that it has caused such lifestyles and patterns of drinking. This should not mean much since the test is to explore pubs in the contemporary situation to see what differences exist between different socioeconomic groups. Let it be said that 'to the great mass of manual workers the local public house spelt paradise .. after the squalor from which so many men came there dwelt within a tavern all that one could crave for - warmth, bright lights, songs, comradeship, smiling condescension of a landlady, large and bosomy, forever sexually unattainable .. but above all men went for the ale that brought a slow fuddled joy. Beer was indeed the shortest way out of city'. (53)

We have now to turn to the last part of chapter two, the recreational, entertainment and sexual licence usages of the public house which we can glean from the dusty pages of history.

Recreation, Entertainment and Sexuality

There is a great deal of evidence about the public house being a source of recreation and fun, relaxation and aetivities and shared interests. Some have suggested that the concept of fun is irreducible, it atomises and disappears. There is also the question of the classical eeonomic theory of class struggle that the struggle for social control was attempted by a rising middle class that owned the means of production and this group sought control of the cultural means of reproduction. This is too deterministic and casually simple for the task attempted here, especially when one considers the work side of the pub and the changing expressions of recreation and sexual freedom.

It appeared there was constant fear in the 1830s of working-class leisure so much so that 'by the 1830s the notion that the movements of the lower orders had comprehensible or legitimate objectives was replaced by the feeling that it aimed somehow at the unravelling of society. Equally the intense interest shown by the middle classes in what the working classes did after their release from the salubrious discipline of mill or workshop, reflected anxiety about the social implications of unsupervised working-class leisure ... the administration of a cultural lobotomy and the implantation of the morally superior lobe went on into the 1850s'. (54) In particular it is claimed that the moral sanitisation process was concerned with control over the 'increasingly covert pub life .. the private foci were suspect .. especially after the Beer House Act of the 1830's and the multiplication of a class of drinking place which could be occupied by extremely humble men .. which encouraged the most abominable sports and games .. the pub served as an aU purpose institution in working-class life', providing more than just drink. It provided 'a house of call, toilet facilities, refuge from the wet and from the wife, dominoes and cards, reading matter, food and drink', whilst 'gambling, prizefighting and demoralising amusements lead to similar attitudes on political questions'. Taking the moralistic attitude out of Storch's claims it is clear that pub life did contain much ofthe then existent leisure activity. (55) What was this culture, where did it come from, how far was it internalised by 'extremely humble men', how far did a community emerge which rejected the 'thinking versus drinking' charge, did these men in accepting the pub see education as a route out, how far was there an identity of interest between the middle classes and working classes because the former preferred 'rational recreation '? How far did the distinct trends of the pre-industrial recreation of sensuality and masculinity become sharpened by the new pub and find an increasing rather than decreasing part to play in the lives of participants? These questions cannot be answered in the abstract nor perhaps historically. There are some hints, namely 'that working men developed their own kind of respectability'. It was a retention of an earthly culture, of an immediate vitality which had 'the bowling, quoiting, glee clubs and free and easies, amateur and professional dramatics, fruit and vegetables shows, sweepstake clubs', but also included the' games, music, getting up country wakes, bull baiting, quoit playing, bowling, wrestling, running, boxing, horse racing, card playing, skittles, Dutch pins, bumble puppy, draughts, dominoes'. (57) It is speculation as to what caused such a process but there is no doubt that two features are outstanding in the range of activities particularised; the emergence of the singing saloons and the link of entertainment to sexual freedom, more colloquially song and sin.

The emergence of singing saloons is illustrated by Rowley (58) and since they were subsequently to lead to the music halls and the professional musician, it is important to know their links to the public drinking house. ' ... musicallife was pub centred, in a period when drink and song appear to have been indissolubly linked ... concert rooms existed in practically every public house ... whenever a licensed place possessed a room capable of holding from thirty people upwards there would be established a free and easy', and 'the entertainment set before saloon audiences was diverse, illustrating the wide resources of popular culture ... they derived from the travelling show and popular theatre, the village green and the street ... the style was boisterous, vulgar and irreverent ... the saloon also had a taste for the spectacle but essential to all performances was the chorus singing, in which the audience came into its own .. the chorus was a compelling ritual that reaffirmed the common identity of its celebrants ... the saloons were particularly disturbing to the reformers .. they saw the brutality and crudeness of the older traditional amusements as excrescences of a folk Of rustic barbarism ... they were now confronted with a thriving institution that was a direct product of modern urban society'. (58) Harrison observes the late nineteenth-century growth and persistence of music halls which evolved from such singing saloons, 'outside London there were at least three hundred in 1868 ... by 1908 there were as many as fifty seven music halls in London.' The music halls became separate from the pub so that, 'here as elsewhere publicans had the initiative to provide a new service, then specialise in it, then lost control of it altogether'. (59) The research which underpins the last section of the book probes the question of how far there is a robust internal public house culture which goes some way to explaining its popularity.

In 1899 in his study of York, Rowntree observes that' .. there can be no doubt that many girls spend their evenings in public houses with a view to meeting men for immoral purposes'. (60) Perhaps men do as well, but he does not make such an observation. As Thompson argues 'animalism might be more preferable to cold and guilty sexuality; while as sexual conduct .. became more inhibited and secretive, so also in great towns, prostitution grew'. (61) There is little doubt that interest in sexuality never left the purvey of the pub. As a reality town life was gregarious and harsh and a locus of diverse activities. There is no reason why it should omit its place as a centre for sexual adventures and personal freedoms, as a Saturday night in Leeds in the I 840s reveals, 'On a Saturday evening, the 24th April, I went to ... visit the low places of resort of the working classes of Leeds ... in almost all there was a sprinkling of professed prostitutes .. .in some ofthese places we found a fiddle or some other instrument being played .. .in another dancing was going on in a good sized room upstairs where I found a dozen couples performing a country dance; the females were all factory girls and prostitutes; obscene attitudes and language accompany and form the chief zest to this amusement .. .in many of these places there was convenience upstairs for the cohabitation of the company below'. (62) As Chesney points out, the link between sexual licence, prostitution and the 'citadels of the underworld' was a strong one with the public drinking house as a context in which the selling of pleasures and fun, easily fostered the selling of much else - including sex for money. (63)

One of the most interesting contemporary aspects relating to sexual usage of the pub is how far men and women use it differently. Research by the OPCS in the late 1970's found that 90% of women would not go into a pub drinking by themselves. Given the loosening of the time framework relating to pub open hours, and the growth of female emancipation, some change may have occurred, just how much change is a matter of empirical enquiry and probing.

Just how far women are emancipated depends upon our definition of men. If we adopt the view that they are the economic, social and sexual achievers, women the recipients, and thus women alone in the public house 'are intruders .. they are made to feel miserable, out of place and unwelcome. The best they can be seen to be doing is waiting for someone; sitting back and relaxing would be a gesture of insolent provocation .. and there is no point in looking to other women to soften the censure .. the escorted women peep out from their secure knot of respectability, conferring with friends with a mixture of compassion and malicious pleasure. I really think that there is nowhere more calculated to make woman alone feel more rejected, paranoid or inept .. the landscape is subtly hostile to the traditional feminine values of domesticity. A pub is another world. It is not meant to be like home. It's the other part of a man's life ... where does a woman alone fit in? If she's not this intruder from the world of domesticity then she is classified as a man hunter'. (64)

The second factor thus in the public house matrix is that if a woman in this context comes alone then she is sexually available. As Ann Whitehead comments 'the pub is a special context promoting dramatic verbal encounters between men and women both because it may provide a licence for behaviour which might not be acceptable in other contexts and because it is associated with sexual availability'. (65) If the pub is a context which posits men as takers of women, women will feel threatened and increasingly so.

It depends on the work routines of women and men and thus the changes which have occurred in the pub will be examined in the light of what happened with work and industrialisation in the next chapter, and breweries concern with trying to be profitable and control the role of the publican in chapter four.

References

1. Bacon, S. D., Alcohol and Complex Society, in Society, Culture and

2. Drinking Patterns, (ed) Pittman and Snyder, pi, Wiley NY 1962

3. The Errol Report on Liquor Licensing, HMSO Cmd 51541972 pl8 3. Cooper D, The Beverage Report op cit, p107

4. Quoted by Jellinet E. M. in Quarterly Journal of Studies on Alcohol, 1940p788.

5. Jellnick E. M. op cit p777

6. World Health Organisation: Expert Committee on Alcohol, 1954

7. Financial Times, 21st March 1979, Special Supplement on Brewing

8. Bradley M. and Fenwick D., OCPS op cit

9. Hutt C., The Death of the English Pub, Arrow Books, 1973 p13.

10. Reynolds M., Prisoner in the Bar, op cit pp 47-48.

  II. Pike E. R., Human Documents of the Industrial Revolution, Allen and Unwin, 1966, p551

12. Smiles S., Character, John Murray, 1877, pp88-92

13. Anthony P. D., The Ideology of Work, Tavistock 1977

14. Webb S. and B., The History of Liquor Licensing in England, London 1903

15. Ibid pp3

16. Ibid pp4-5

17. Ibid p22

18. Ibid p2l

19. Ibid piS

20. Smollett T., History of England, Vol. 11, Chapter 18, p430, published London 1848

21. Webb S. and B., op cit, p68

22. Ibid p72

23. Ibid pp 50-51.

24. Ibid p. 50-51.

25. Ibid p. 50-51.

26. Bailey P., Leisure and Class in Victorian England, Routledge and Kegan Paul,. 1978 P.9.

27. Monckton H. A., A. History of the English Public House, Bodley Head 1969, p.78.

28. Webb S. and B., op cit, pp 118-119.

29. Ibid pp 123-125.

30. Bailey p. op cit p.29.

31. Ibid p.1l3.

32. Monckton H. A., op cit p.83.

33. Ibid p.84

34. Bailey P. op cit p. 174.

35. Extracted from H. A. Monckton op cit.

36. Bailey P. op cit.

37. Marcuse H. essay on, The Alternative Character of Culture, in Negations, Allen Lane 1969 p.98.

38. Quoted by Monckton H. A. op cit.

39. Bailey P. op cit pp 15-16.

40. Ibid p.l6

41. Ibid p.lO.

42. Harrison B., op cit p.313.

43. Harrison B. op cit p.169.

44. Ibid p.169.

45. Bailey P., op cit pp15-16

46. Chesney K., The Victorian Underworld, Temple Press, London 1970, pp91-92

47. Pike E. R., Human Documents of the Industrial Revolution, Allen and

48. Unwin, 1965 p31 0

49. Chesney K., op cit ppl06-107 and 194

50. Harrison B., op cit, pl72

51. Quoted in P. Bailey op cit p9 London J., The People ofthe Abyss, Nelson, 1903

52. Thompson E. P., The Making of The English Working Class, Victor Gollanz, 1963 pp57-58

53. Roberts R., The Classic Slum, Manchester University Press, 1971, pp93-94

54. Storch R. D., The Problems of Working Class Leisure, Some Roots of Middle Class Reform in the Industrial North 1825-1850, in Social Control in 19C Britain, ed by Donajgrodkl, Croom Helm 1977

55. Ibid pl41

56. Rowley J. 1., Drink and the Public House in Nottinghamshire 1830-60, in Transactions of the Thornton Society of Nottinghamshire Vol. LXXIX 1975 p76

57. Quoted by 1. J. Rowley op cit p79

58. Bailey P. op cit pp31-34

59. Harrison B., op cit p 179

60. Rowntree B. S., Poverty: A Study of Town Life in York in 1899, published London, 1901 p312

61. Thompson E. P., op cit p413

62. Cited by E. R. Pike op cit pp292-293

63. Chesney K., The Victorian Underworld, op cit pp196-7

64. Garvey A., Women in Pubs, in New Society 21st February 1974, pp459-460

65. Ann Whitehead, Sexual Antagonism in Hertfordshire, p183 in Dependence and Exploitation in Work and Marriage, (ed) Barker D.L. and Allen s., Longman, 1976

Chapter 3
Work and the
Culture of the Public House

In the new millennium , work is central in our society. We are often reminded of the importance of work, of the necessity for qualificaions, of the economic value of high paid employment, of the 'well being' that a career can bring. We are encouraged to put work demands first in our thinking, and everything else is second. At least the central official impression is that not to work means not to eat, thus we ought to view work as the central core of life's experience. (1)

There are a host of questions relating to the structure and meaning of work. Yet if we simply approach the public house from this perspective, we again will end up with lots of clues and insights. To a large extent we will put the pub on the fringes of our enquiry, as a dependent variable, rather than viewing it as central and independent. We will however be making a judgement in the second part of the book about what the public house means. What does it do for its many users? How do those who are unemployed use their pub? Do the self-employed or professionals use the pub in the same way? Do they use the same pub? Does our age and sex make differences to how we use the public house? Basically, the central issue is not to become overwhelmed by turning history on its head, if one views the public house as pivotal in the intermix of social factors. It is rather like picking up the net with various leads from the point where one picks it up - thus if the public drinking house is the central point of analysis, one arrives at different viewing perspectives - perspectives that have interesting conclusions which must await the findings of the research.

The fact of paid employment, and how it changed in to timed labour and efficiency, is the question we have to pursue. It is worthwhile bearing in mind that the lifestyles surrounding the public house were not unpatterned and unorganised, but rather their coherence were of a different mode, to some extent focused by the oppressiveness of mechanised work demands, but hardly caused by them. The economic ethic and its compatibility with 'natural work rhythms' will be one issue examined.

A second issue which is of concern is the current situation regarding work as timed labour and efficiency - is there still a conflict? This is a claim to cast our net so that we gain the insights of occupational groups and leisure, family and gender sociability patterns.

So in what ways and with what consequences did the public house stand in direct opposition to the increasing tyranny of work, with the timing and mechanised efficiency so characteristic of the labour market? Not all argued that it was the enforced idleness which 'drove the youth to the pot-house and the girls to the brothel'. (2) To put Lenin and Marx more totally in their context, 'On Saturday evenings, especially when wages are paid ... the whole working class pours from its own poor quarters into the thoroughfare, intemperance may be seen in all its brutality ... next to intemperance in the enjoyment of intoxicating liquors, one of the principal faults of English working men is sexual licence .. the failings of the workers in general may be traced to an unbridled thirst for pleasure'. (3) In classic economic class theory, the cause was the bourgeoisie who owned the means of production, therefore 'it is self evident that the labourer is nothing else, his whole life through, than labour power, that therefore all his disposable time is by nature and law, labour time, to be devoted to the self expansion of capital'. (4) It is a pity that the assumed dominance of work, and instructive pose for the unbridled thirst for pleasure, may have little to do with the power of capital, ownership of the means of production or quest for surplus value. It may have a lot to do with human resistance to the constraints imposed by machine driven work routines, and extrinsically derived patterns of time and activity. These are features of most economic organisation. In short these early exponents of a class theory have done what has been suggested one ought to take care about, treating work as the independent variable. The preference for intemperance and sexual licence may be preferred; pleasure and gregariousness and sociability may be important in human choices and activities. We have to answer the question of how tyrannous was this process. How, and how far did the mechanisation of labour and time usage of human effort, fit in with public house time patterns and the hedonistic materialism, sensuality and masculinity of its culture? The process of 'industrialisation is like a landscape which has blasted by ... moral drought; one must travel through many tens of thousands of words of parched historical abstraction between each oasis of human actuality'. (5) To put the issue rather directly, 'how far and in what ways did this shift in time affect labour discipline, and how far does it influence the inward apprehension of time of working people?' (5) And is there any direct relationship to the formidable social controls identified by the 'magistrates, mill owners and methodists' in the preceding chapter?

The dramatic, but by no means all pervasive, change brought about in the organisation of work was the shift from natural work rhythms which are ones own, typified by sense of work time which is task oriented, to that of timed labour regulated by machine rhythms. It was this shift from personal task to machine oriented time which was the radical change that occurred in the Victorian period.

Thompson suggests there are three important features of natural work rhythms: 'First, there is the sense in which it is more humanly comprehensible than timed labour. The peasant or labourer appears to attend upon what is observed necessity. Second, a community in which task orientation is common appears to show least demarcation between work and life. Social intercourse and labour are intermingled ... there is no great sense of conflict between labour and passing the time of day. Third, to men accustomed to labour time by the clock, this attitude appears wasteful and lacking in urgency'. (6) The pure form of the integration of the task oriented labourer or peasant worker is the independent craftsman, the highly-skilled worker who works for themselves on a specific job or task. However it is clearly not the typical mode of dependant status, the worker under capitalism was in an employed dependant status, thus 'the historical record is not a simple one of neutral and inevitable technological change but also one of exploitation and resistance to exploitation ... what needs to be said is not one way of life is better than the other, but this is a place of most far reaching conflict'. (7) The conflict which took place, and to some extent still exists via the mobile phones, the computerised access and the CCTV recordings, poses the same conflict, namely this obsession with economic efficiency and an employment relationship based upon a cash nexus as a capitalist form of economic organisation. And probably the conflict is far deeper and more extensive than ever anticipated. The poverty and precariousness of the Victorian life, the attempt to change the traditional non-work values and import them into the mechanised work context, the attempt to impose a civilising morality on the beer sodden culture, suggest that the change was not very successful or so ambivalent that the public house modernised and changed its format so that it retained its appeal. The shift from a task-based to a mechanised-based production system was dependent upon the growth of the factory system - a system we variously have to the present day, a system which required 'the time sheet, the time keeper, the informer and fines .. we are concerned simultaneously with time-sense in its technological conditioning, and time measurement as a means of labour exploitation'. (8) It was not so much that a different order of working was required but also a different attitude to work itself was needed, instead of the whole person being employed they were taken on as' ... part human beings, soulless, depersonalised, disembodied, who could become members or little wheels of a complex mechanism. It was that men who were non-accumulative, non-acquisitive, accustomed to work for subsistence, not for maximisation of income, had to be made obedient to the cash nexus'. (9) Such obedience was difficult to obtain indeed against a tradition which emphasised song, sin and sensuality, which was naturalistic rather than rational, which did take the public house as part of a continuing framework of life, so much so the workers evidenced 'the utmost distaste on the part of the men to do any regular hours .. the men were considerably dissatisfied because they could not go in and out as they pleased, and have what holidays they pleased, and go on just as they had been used to'. (10) The factory meant economy of time, in the Webb's phrase 'enforced asceticism', so much so that 'bad timekeeping was punished by severe fines and it was common in mills ... to lock the gates of the factory, even the workroom, excluding those who were only a minute or two late'. (11)

It was the interdependence of the division of labour which characterised the mills, and later the factories, which imposed time discipline so that workers could not just simply down their tools and join in the local fox hunt Of chase, or resort to the pot house or beer shop. As Pollard notes, Wedgewood as an early manufacturer amongst others, had to fight the old pottery tradition by introducing the 'punctuality, constant attendance, the fixed hours, the scrupulous standards of care and cleanliness, the avoidance of waste, and the bar on drinking'. (12) Arkwright, and James Watt, engaged in similar conflicts to change the attitudes and behaviour of their workers. Steam power and the growth of the factory system resulted in an accompanying philosophy oftime thrift. New attitudes were required to accompany the timed labour of a rigorous system. 'Mechanisation meant the need for a sober, predictable labour force .. the inseparability of drinking from customary recreation made it difficult to obtain precise and regular workmanship, yet these were the qualities required by the factory system. The ancient inseparability of work and recreation patterns, had to change'. (13) By the 1870s the change was almost complete, so 'the first generation of factory workers were taught by their masters the importance of time, the second generation formed their short time committee in the ten hour movement, the third generation struck for overtime or time and a half ... they had well learned the lesson that time means money'. (14) The conflict between work in the work place and leisure in the pub, between routinised labour time and a self regulated and integrated work and play syndrome, is vividly at the heart of the history of 'Saint Monday'. Reid's account of Birmingham between 1766 and 1866, forcibly demonstrates the case argued here, that industrial work values and time were increasingly in conflict with popular cultures and life-styles, and this conflict focused around the public drinking house. Thus 'as a matrix of small workshops the town formed a conducive environment for the survival of immemorial work rhythms ... the water milling of metal was central to the town's prosperity but seasonal variations in the supply of water tended to reinforce uneven patterns of application to work ... the demands of the clock were often yet subordinated to the desire for sociability'. The tradition of ritualistic withdrawal from work on

Mondays was penetrated by a pot-house and tavern culture, by drinking and games: 'reveals the alehouse as a primary venue, and drink, bar games and the entertainment of various sorts the primary pastime. Out of doors the most prominent sports were pugilism and animal fights ... up to the late 1830s dog fights used to happen every Monday ... and there used to be some cock fighting carried out on almost every Monday afternoon in public houses in and around town'. Thus by 1840, Monday was 'generally kept as a holiday by a great portion of the working classes'. The struggle between labour time discipline and the lifestyles of the working class, focused around the tavern or public house, typified by Saint Monday, fundamentally changed with the introduction of steam power so that by 1864 the tradition Reid argues, was vulnerable, 'the fundamental reason .. was the application of steam power to hardware production. Only in the mid nineteenth century did Birmingham significantly emulate the cotton industry in its use of steam and only then did Saint Monday become truly vulnerable'. The conflict became intense and obvious: 'The capitalist wished for the most efficient employment of his investment .. the worker wished to defend his way of life'. Reid concludes that the Saint Monday tradition was as much eroded as demolished and 'such erosion resulted from the trade-off by manufacturers and owners, of sobriety and regular workers on Monday for a half-day's holiday on Saturday'. (15) Playing away on Mondays, was the kind of situation described by Disraeli in Wodgate where 'the men seldom exceed four days of labour in a week. On Sunday, the master workmen begin to drink, for apprentices there is dog fighting without stint. On Monday and Tuesday the whole population is drunk .' here is relaxation and excitement'. (16)

The changes in work discipline, and the shift towards timed labour cannot be easily separated from what was happening elsewhere to control the behaviour of the undermass. As indicated in the previous chapter, constraints on alcohol consumption were pervasive after 1870 both in terms of licensing laws and limits to recreation and lifestyles.

As Thompson indicates: <the division of labour, the supervision of labour, bells and clocks, money incentives, preaching and schooling, suppression of fairs and sports - new labour habits were formed and a new time discipline imposed .. and we may doubt how far it was ever fully accomplished .. throughout the nineteenth century the propaganda of time thrift continued to be directed at the working people'. (17)

The historical evidence supports the view that in terms of work time and the increasing proportion of lifestyles focused around work, there is still a complex and formidable array of evidence. Just how invariable this is when one actually interviews people and looks at the options they have, their life situation and the work and lifestyles they display, the techno-rationalist tradition may reveal significant failings. Also changes in work itself, particularly the fact that much work is now in the service sector, and many women are imploding against the employment glass ceiling, have changed the situation significantly, and have also influenced the public drinking house.

Work and Public Health

The claim that drinking caused ill health is a complex one. The literature is such that one could disappear down the rabbit hole and never be seen again. Several caveats are relevant thus; much of the analysis separates the social meanings from the social contexts of drinking, something this analysis has refused to do. Much of the material is based on a deterministic, biological analysis of the unconstrained social consequences of drinking, very much a minority problem. Finally much of the material does rest upon a moralistic and paternalistic social health approach, such as to give rise to a resuscitated spectre of licensing legislation as described in the preceding chapter.

By a vigorous application of the economic and moral discipline the conflict between 'pot-house culture' and work regulated time had been resolved. Such an impression distorts the evidence, particularly when 'the condition of England' problem was linked with the asserted social costs, such that in 190 I it was claimed that 'so long as the vice of intemperance remains what it is today, so long will the utmost efforts of the political economist be hindered and thwarted .. .it would be an epoch in which there was no waste ... of human lives, no ignoble sloth, above all no waste of health, substance and self respect in drunkenness, and its attendant vices'. The problems associated with the public house and drinking had not gone away, if anything the effect had been to reinforce some aspects of drinking behaviour, thus 'the conditions of labour are still extremely irksome, and often painfully exacting. Introduction of the factory system and the more extensive use of machinery, while they have lessened the physical burden of work, have added to it nervous tension and extreme monotony .. if added to these conditions the incessant noise and whirr of machinery, the noxious heat and dust-laden air of the workshops and factories, and the close and continuous confinement, the attractiveness of the public house in the hours of relaxation can easily be recognised'. The restrictions placed on the public house aiming to bring it under control by 'magistrates, mill owners and methodists' in the nineteenth century, the policy of 'enforced', so a 'sober labour force' existed, was clearly only partially successful. As work became reorganised and regimented the pub became an increasing focus of drinking and alcohol consumption, thus the social problem became how to reduce alcohol and to do so by making the public house less attractive in itself. The social reformers sought to promote cultural and rational recreation. The analysis of the' drink problem' being amenable to 'rational recreation' was not new but the proportion - going by alcohol and mortality figures alone - combined with such slogans as 'Public Health is Public Wealth' concentrated attention with living standards and the health of the labour force. Such concern effectively incorporated a work ethic into a 'social efficiency' of more general applicability, ' ... to win as many as possible away from the opposing delights of the drinking shops'. Such moralistic aims meant, 'physical refreshment and rational recreation of the working classes .. the public house question is an "entertainment of people" question .. .the reformation so undoubtedly and imperatively demanded must, to be really effective, take the shape of a complete reconstruction of our public house system .. consumption of intoxicants in the UK is at present so excessive as to be dangerous to morality, prosperity and health'. The link was thus made between something more than recreation, it was between recreation and 'the question of industrial supremacy'. Thus the reformers wanted' Peoples Palaces' in which 'rational recreation could be combined with full opportunity for cheerful intercourse and healthy stimulus', through exhibitions, concerts, arts and crafts schemes, gymnasia and 'bright and cheerful clubs for working lads and working girls', so as to produce 'character and fitness for citizenship'.

The ultimate claim was to add to the already existing legal, religious, and work constraints upon the public house, the ultimate state control and a social castration of the public drinking house such that, 'no female bar tenders would be employed, no adventitious attractions such as music would be associated with sale of intoxicants. Accommodation for clubs, sick benefit societies, etc. would no longer be provided at public houses ... every public house would be open to full public inspection from the highway. Back door and side entrances would no longer be provided'. (18) Drinking and the Public House fostered irrational behaviour, undermined public health, and threatened the civilising aims of economic achievement and the moral order.

Work and Understanding the Pub

It will be useful to be brought up to date and deal with the contemporary situation, thus we will deal with work, sociability and the public house, and it is worth bearing in mind a number of things; that manufacturing is less a part of the total economy than it was, the factory and machine is sympathetically run by the computer, that women in Britain have the highest proportion of work in any European country, and brewers have helped to run their pubs more commercially by selling their products outside of them, and have moved into hotels, clubs, restaurants and discos.

How far does the pub relate to the work situation of the contemporary worker? The quest for 'reward without effort' still exists, but fairly severe licensing restrictions back up the demands of economic efficiency and rational striving for supposedly obtainable objectives. How far is work still experienced as a quest for economising efficiency? What is proposed is that manual and non-manual occupations may have become less different in this respect than in the past, but an important divide may persist in terms of the sociability patterns which find expression in how the pub is used. The contemporary situation is one where the inhuman hours of earlier periods, as well as major changes in the structure of the labour force itself, have occurred. It would be facile to offer a snapshot of work time and values characteristic of contemporary society. However, there are several indicators worthy of consideration which in themselves point to major changes.

The first important factor is the still undoubted hardness and triviality of much paid employment as timed labour. Production and efficiency are not vacuous concepts, and employment for many manual and non-manual occupations has still the feeling of emptiness and desolation, 'I dread the fact of going in day after day; it's the same routine. You stand in one place ... there's no end to it' . (19) The purposelessness of work is added to by the necessity of producing against the clock, on a piece-work basis, a characteristic of much manual employment, as Jackson suggests: 'there was no other judgement than the speed of working .. the pace of work was uncomfortably fast ... time rates were unattainable'. (20) The twin of monotony and pace of work are most characterised in assembly-line technology which results in 'highly fragmented and repetitive tasks with little intrinsic satisfaction'. (21) The time of the assembly line may be past with the introduction of computerised technology, and the reformation of the work group, but still the tyranny of timed labour, and the stress upon becoming 'efficient' still operates in 'cash nexus' of employment. Much has been done to explain in occupational community studies how work, play and sociability are locked together. Some manual work is not timed in the factory sense. The study by Hollowell of lorry drivers and Sykes study of Navvies shows the extent to which there are attempts to retain freedom, this figures significantly in the work and life styles of manual workers. (22)

Another clue to the enigma of generalising from the narrow base of a production framework is the evidence from within the system by those who attempt to control such constraints, the workers themselves. Fixing the piece rate system, extensive fiddling and the social practices underpinning absenteeism are strategies of independence used by time-labour, so that' .. .in spite of the alleged slowness of machines, or excessively fast rates, everyone always earned the maximum bonus. To achieve this men 'fiddled' the amount of work entered on their time sheets until it agreed with the time for the job. Fiddling took various forms depending on the work process'. (23)

There are many occupations which have been studied and do not adhere to clock driven time and which illustrate the co-operative nature of fiddling and fixing. At one level it is a time-effort reward equation, an effort to increase monetary income. However as is made clear by Jackson, such resistance is embedded in event-driven lifestyles and values, 'suspicion intensified because piece-work made everyone not workmates but competitors. Management sought productivity ... the workforce reacted by using their own weapons. Since overtime was compulsory, and work hours bore no relation to the rest of their interests and responsibilities, they earned high wages for a number of days, then took a day off and spent it sleeping, or bowling in the park or sitting in the club .. a second defence set up by work people was rate fixing ... successive alterations to the piece-rates only produced a kind of busy standing still ... they tried to impose an action on the assumption that middle-class life was normal life and working-class life only a problem variant'. Jackson discusses in detail the factors which make clock time and working-class community, 'the man has nothing to live for except his labour and his skill'. The threat of poverty is relieved when the children begin to work but that 'passes, once children leave home there begins the slow drop into the poverty band again 'n this deep and terrible rhythm is the very ground of working-class life'. The experience of hard times gives rise to the importance of mutuality and is characteristic of the clubs, pubs and sociable groupings so much part of working- class life. Such is reinforced by the traditional close linkage between work and neighbourhood, so that income and work become reinforced by living in one class neighbourhoods. The kinship ties 'based more on where mothers and daughters want to live than on what men might want to do' , create the extended families both obsessively analysed by sociologists and misunderstood by social workers and planners. Jackson castigates these last two groups but pinpoints the restructuring of community caused by rehousing 'the most serious challenge to the old patterns .. .the enormous rehousing of the working class .. a huge number of which [houses] are in council estates on city outskirts replacing the working-class districts near the centre. Almost all of this work has been carried out in complete ignorance of the styles of life ... community centres are no substitute for community'. The importance which Jackson emphasises is the link between clock time as timed labour, and the culture and lifestyle of the working classes. Resistance is that of 'vitality within fatalism' to use his phrase. (24) The clue he offers to the link between work and use of the public house is an important one. Lifestyles characterised by an event or episodic approach to time, in which situations become incidents, and in which mutuality is reinforced by the harshness of labour, are questionably caused by such experiences. Does this resistance still find expression in the public house as a focus of sociability? Also, as important, what modes of adjustment in the new areas without pubs, or with 'improved' pubs, now exist?

There is no claim that work is the cause of how men and women take life's opportunities, since 'social life has an obdurate complexity which can be counted upon to badly dent, if not demolish most .. concepts that are unlucky enough to make contact with it'. (25)

Does the usage of the public house deserve, along with the people who use it, a more generous definition than posed by Harrison and Bailey in the previous chapter? The initial stance adopted here is very much the position adopted, that 'many of the influences of work upon leisure are permissive rather than deterministic .. many work-based 'causes' are translated into specific leisure effects through independent mediating processes. Besides being workers, individuals are involved in other social relationships and immersed in other sources of values ... the sum of the evidence does not justify treating leisure as a purely dependent variable .. while it may be one crucial element, work is not the only source of contemporary man's consciousness and identity'. (26)

Some discussion has been about manual workers' clock time or time thrift approach to work, as opposed to a organic naturalistic or events approach, but what of non-manual workers and professionals. How has their situation changed? Is the public house the basis for their recreation and free time? Do professional women have the same attitudes as men? There are some fragmentary clues, albeit related to their availability, the empirical content of which will be examined in later chapters. The 'non-manual' category of occupations conceals a range of work - from the black-coated worker to the highly-skilled professional. Lockwood's classic analysis offers some clues to the former category when compared to the mid-nineteenth century, thus: 'the black coat of the mid-nineteenth century clerk symbolised his middle-class status ... running then this sartorial claim to status was the social gulf between the manual worker and the rest. Working with one's hands was associated with other attributes - lack of authority, illiteracy, lowly social origins, insecurity of livelihood - which together spelt deprecation. The dominant values were those of the entrepreneurial and professional middle class ... the practical result was that of the exclusion of the manual wage earner from middle-class society'. Lockwood proceeds to explore the market situation and status of the clerk and reveals the post-1945 pressure to redefine the occupation, 'the clerk is an unskilled labourer under modern conditions [so that] productivity has acquired the universal and disinterested appeal of the common norm'. (27) The suggestion is that clearly the market situation and status of the clerk have 'declined', but other occupations are more difficult, there are differences which accelerate towards the top end of the professional hierarchy. In such professional occupations the individual is much more able to negotiate, substitute and transpose the constraints which work imposes. The kind and degree of work may well be a better distinction than the manual- non-manual one. 'Any consideration of the rewards and deprivation of work must be concerned with more than just the obvious financial rewards and should see the part which subordination and loss of autonomy play as part of the costs of working which can [also] vary considerably between different work situations'. One could argue here that freedom in work results in freedom out of work, that autonomy in work may influence the ways sociability out of work is crucially interdependent, especially when usage of the public house is examined. What is possible is to examine in depth the time constraints in work and the 'time free' context of sociability. Also what differences, if any, exist in the ways in which the public house is used by different participants in relation to timed labour in work? Are there differences between working and middle- class usages which result in ways in which work, sociability and friendships network? If there are such differences do they result in usage differences between the public houses as well as within them? Some of these questions can only be answered by research, but there are pointers in the analysis, explored by Allan, in his linking of sociability and friendship patterns. There is considerable evidence, suggests Allan, that 'whereas the middle class develop their friendships through recognising the possibility of interaction in a variety of social settings, the working class tend far more to limit their sociable relations to particular social contexts and structures. They do allow them to "flower out" in the way the middle class do'.

Allan shows the kind of integration whereby, 'workmates are normally leisure time companions, often neighbours, and not infrequently kinsmen .. the values expressed through the social networks emphasise mutual aid in everyday life and the obligation to join in the gregarious pattern of leisure, in a public and present oriented conviviality'. This is a situation capable of numerous interpretations, particularly the influence of occupation on working-class versus middle-class pub usage patterns. Allan suggests that the classes possessed different 'rules of relevance' for both sociability and friendship patterns, thus the 'rules of relevance which shape sociable relationships emphasise the personal relationship, whatever the social setting in which it occurs, for the middle class, but affirms the primacy of the interactionable setting in which the relationships develop for the working class ... the working class were much more likely to define the activity as the primary rationale for a sociable relationship existing at all'. The net result, suggests Allan, is that social relationships and friendship patterns for the working class are more locality specific and situation specific, and thus are much more segmented, than middle class patterns. He rejects the rosy image presented by Jackson and others claiming that the dominant pattern of working class community is 'somewhat removed from that assumed in the literature on the traditional worker'. Importantly Allan points out that the working-class do not use their homes as a basis of sociability. Insofar as they maintain friendship patterns they tend tohave 'mates' tied to particular situational settings, rather than friendships which cross cut role networks. Just how this interacts in Allan's research is as follows, particularly 'mate relationships deny a central tenet of friendship, that the individual rather than activity is central ... the mate relationship also differs from middle-class friend relationships in that it can be group based ... group sociability of this form [is] a recurrent feature of male working-class sociable patterns [and] derives its character from interaction defined as consequent on joint participation in specific settings, particularly patronage of the same pub ... the group emerges from setting and is largely confined to it. In other words people go to the pub for a drink not simply or solely to meet particular others but in the knowledge that they will find people they know and enjoy meeting'. Allan concludes that it is the home that is used by the middle class to transcend particular structures and situations, while it is outside home entertainment for the working class which makes it more likely that relationships will be situationally specific. (28)

Three conclusions may be derived from Allan's study: Firstly that the working class now, in addition to the tyranny of labour, have a reason for using the public house, it is the use of it as a non-home base for activity with their mates, as a private situation of public interaction; secondly that the middle class will use the pub as a place to take friends, as a context for the public situation of private interaction; thirdly if the situation is like this it would explain non usage by women, alone or in groups, even given the growth by women of their involvement, where men often see them as predatory or outcasts.

It is easier to pose questions than to answer them. However to pose such questions is not from the position of 'using the rhetoric and models of the neat logico-deductive formal theories as a substitute for data'. (29) We have to 'line up what one takes as theoretically possible with what one is finding in the field. Such existing sources of insights are to be cultivated, though not at the expense of insights generated by the qualitative research, which are still closer to the data'. (30)

Conclusion

We have threaded our way through the claims of the various theorists who have tried to 'put the lid' on the public house. From a careful analysis the demands of 'clock time' have increasingly been onerous, and when viewed within the framework of the nineteenth-century restrictions on premises, on drinking at work, on licensing, on the fun and games which the pub generates, they were subject to severe restraints. We also perceived the difficulties which the modern writer had in knowing what the pub did, what service it offered and what part it had to play in our contemporary society. There was no doubt about the time constraint of work, of greater choices the individual freedoms between roles. Situational segmentation seemed to characterise the workingclass usage. Both working and middle class seemed increasingly to use the pub, but in different ways. After examining the role of the brewers and the essential publicans' role we will turn to the climax - what different types of users think of their public houses.

Chapter 3 References

1. See especially, Michael A Smith, Doctor of Philosophy Thesis, London School of Economics, 'Protestant Asceticism and Working Class Conviviality', Appendix 10, 1981

2. Marx K., Capital: A Critique of Political Economy, Vol. 1. p.252, Lawrence and Wishart, London, 1954

3. Engels F., The Conditions of the Working Classes in England, Lawrence and Wishart, London, 1973, pp147-l49

4. Ibid pl46

5. Anthony P.O., in The Ideology of Work, Tavistock, London 1977

6. Thompson, E.P., Time, Work Discipline and Industrial Capitalism, in Past and Present, No. 38, 1967, p60

7. Ibid pp60-94

8. Pollard S., Factory Discipline in the Industrial Revolution, in Economic History Review, Vol. XVI, 1963 p.254.

9. Ibid p254

10. Ibid p255

11. Ibid p257

12. Ibid p258

13. Harisson B., Drink and the Victorians, Faber and Faber 1971, p40 See also Dunlop J., The Philosophy of Artificial and Compulsory Usage in Great Britain and Ireland, Houlston and

Stoneman, London, 1839

14. Thompson E.P., op cit, p86

15. Reid, D.A., The Decline of Saint Monday, 1766-1876, in Past and Present, No.71, 1976, p77

16. Disraeli, B., Sybil, or the Two Nations, Macmillan, London 1895, pl78

17. Thompson E.P., op cit, p90

18. Rowntree 1. and Sherwell A., The Temperance Problem and Social Reform, 9th edn., Hodder and Stoughton, 1901

19. Kornhauser A., Mental Health and Industrial Worker, Wiley, New York, 1965, plOl

20. Jackson B., Working Class Community, Routledge and Kegan Paul, 1968,p94

21. Parker S .R. and Smith M.A. et al, The Sociology of Industry, Allen and Unwin, 1977, p96

22. Hollowell, P.G., The Lorry Driver, Routledge and Kegan Paul, 1968, also Sykes A.J.M., Navvies; Their Social Relations, in Sociology No.3, 1969,ppl57-172

23. Jackson B., op cit, p96

24. Ibid pp148-163

25. Lockwood D., In Search of the Traditional Worker, P239 in Bulmer M., (ed), Working Class Images of Society, Routledge, 1975

26. Roberts K., Contemporary Society and the Growth of Leisure, Longman, 1978 p113-123

27. Lockwood D., The Blackcoated Worker, Allen and Unwin, 1958, pp99105

28. Allan G., A Sociology of Friendship and Kinship, Allen and Unwin, 1979, pp70-89

29. Glaser B. and Stauss A., The Discovery of Grounded Theory, Weidenfeld and Nicholson, 1967 p91

30. Ibid p253

Chapter 4

The Brewer and the Brewing Industry

The brewing industry is submerged in the mists of time. This does make it difficult to deal with. Part anecdotal, part historical, being wrapped in a strange mix of social movements, issues which are important for the moment. But behind these issues are the ways of life of ordinary people, and that which occurred in their lives, they are momentous in that they affected the lives of men and women, how they lived, the opportunities they had, the freedoms and constraints they experienced.

It was not so much that work influenced the changes which occurred over the period from 1830 to the present day, 'social historians studying nineteenth century England tend to concentrate on the work situation and therefore on the conflicting interests of employer and' employee ... the popular basis of nineteenth-century liberalism brings into the forefront quite different social alignments. Popular liberalism was the product of the leisure of Saturday night and Sunday morning, the pot house and the chapel, not the working week ... there is no comprehensive scholarly work on the brewing industry between 1830 and 1886 ... on the role of drink, drink sellers and the drink interests in society'. (1) To some extent, Harrison's own detailed probing, has remedied the situation, particularly his penetrating analysis of Drink and the Victorians. (2) The strength of the drink interest in the pre-I 870 period derived from two main elements, the extent to which it was closely integrated into most aspects of a rural economy, and the persisting links between economic transactions and recreation.

Given that there is a close link between the brewers and their pubs, and that over 90% of on-licensed premises are now in breweries ownership (3), the trend is towards fewer and bigger companies which was clearly evident by the 1870s.

Harrison suggests the first connection was between the rural economy and distilling and was an intimate one, so that 'publicans and brewers were often substantial landowners; beer and grain prices fluctuated together ... malt cattle feed was as important to the farmer, as the manure obtained from the distillery and innkeepers' stables. London butchers stocked up from cattle fed on grain from London distilleries ... the structure of drink manufacture and sale demanded close co-operation with many brewers ... often invested surplus capital in other trades. The seasonal character of the brewing industry forced brewers into the banking and corn dealing worlds during the inactive summer months ... brewers and bankers were often the only wealthy tradesmen in a community. Much of the capital financing industrialisation came from the food industry ... the rich banked with the drink manufacturers just as the poor banked with the drink retailers'. (4) The link between brewers, landed wealth, banking and finance capital is an established one. (5) Brewers were often themselves magistrates and their lifestyles moved in the social circles of the rich and powerful, as the Times noted in 1827 the brewer magistrate was a 'man of immense wealth, [with] a splendid mansion in the country and a park crowded with deer'. (6) Secondly, brewers were prominent in large-scale philanthropy and thus controlled substantial charity funds and powers of social patronage. Thirdly, there was the fact that wine merchants were often personal advisers to the aristocracy - thus prestige was added to influence and power. It is little wonder that the huge London breweries symbolised industrial greatness. 'Industrial wealth, landed interest, social prestige and influence made the drink interest formidable but more so because of the interest of public authorities in the drink trade, the magistrates and municipal council at local level and the treasury at national level. Liquor taxes contributed over one third of national revenues as late as 1900 ... powerful on committees administering poor relief, closely supervising local licensing regulations, influential on most local authority committees, the drink interest was a powerful one'. (7) There seemed little doubt that such a major penetration and perpetuation of economic interests would result in the consolidation of a powerful grouping of brewery ownership and brewing monopoly. The 1830 Beer House Act creating beer shops, was aimed at establishing a healthier drink - beer rather than gin - but by the 1880s had begun to lead to rapid disappearance of the independent retail brewery, and the dominance of a fast consolidation of brewery oligopoly interests. Part of the explanation lies in the increasingly restrictive local authority health controls over the product and process of production, in a rapidly expanding market. The sheer growth of population during the period, and the difficulties of ensuring the non-adulteration and 'keeping of beer , , when added to the cost-benefits of economies of scale - mass production in a mass market - almost ensured the disappearance of independent brewing and the individual retail brewer. As one writer observed: 'the nineteenth century marked a rapid decline of private brewing because it was becoming less economic to brew at home or on the estate. In round figures private brewing accounted for about half the consumption at the beginning of the century [1800]; and by the end of it had almost dwindled to nothing' . (8) Large-scale brewing, to cope with the expanding market, required capital investment in large-scale plant and that effectively ensured a concentration of production in fewer hands. The rise and fall of the retail brewers indicates the trend, thus 'in 1830 there were 1,269 registered, by 1839 there were 18,017, by 1880 numbers had fallen back to

6,157 and by 1914 to 880'. (9-11) The need for meeting' a mass demand for a mass market', was only one factor shaping the brewers' interests. It was most obviously reinforced by the increasingly imposed rigorous licensing requirements imposed on the public house. The legal constraints on the fitness of premises, persons to run them, activities permitted, hours of opening, categories of persons to be served - all aided the development of a tied house system. The tied house system seems to have been consolidated as the solution between the publican and brewer. The necessity for the purchase and improvement of a public house, and fitness of the person, were guaranteed by the brewer, whilst the house was tied to the brewer's product. Such benefits coincided with the social objectives of usage overtly agreed by the local justices, 'a wholesome usage in a wholesome environment'. The particular nature of the tied house is dealt with later in this chapter, but this establishment of the tied house was a growing feature of the brewing industry after 1870. The trend was towards 'fewer and bigger companies', and Baxter points out that by 1910, nearly half the beer output was produced by forty seven firms, of which the ten largest produced 25% of total output. An examination of barrel age in 1880 compared to 1914 shows the considerable shrinkage in the number of small brewers.

Breweries	Barrels	1880	1914
Producing	'000's		
	Under 1	16,770	2,536
	1-10	1,768	1,188
	10 - 20	272	197
	20-100	203	280
	100 - 500	23	46
	500+	4	8

Source: Baxter J., The Organisation of the Brewing Industry, unpublished PhD thesis, University of London, 1945.

The period between 1880 and 1914 merits the description of one of the 'Brewers Wars', since while the pre-1880 period witnessed' ... the use of steam, the ability to safely construct large vessels, and more precise methods of control over the brewing process. The large commercial brewers gradually displaced publican brewers and domestic brewers ... the bigger brewers grew faster and thus their growth was accentuated by improvements in transport, the growth of urban conglomeration and the increasing mechanisation of the brewing process', the 1880-1914 period saw these trends added to by several others; the most important of these was the growth of the joint stock market which gave access to investment capital. There were capital gains to be made from share issues, and there was an opportunity to find money on a scale to finance considerable expansion .. this Stock Exchange boom became the basis for a scramble for licensed property'. (10) The "war" for control over retail licensed premises so that "the Brewers Society estimated that the percentage of tied property had risen from over 70% to 95% of total licenses". What made such competition over ownership of public houses fierce and essential to large brewery was what was happening elsewhere. You had increasingly restrictive policies of magistrates and the substantial increase in population thus 'from 1886 to 1914 the number of on-licenses fell from 104,792 to 88,445 in England and Wales while the population increased from 1881 to 1911 by 44%. (11)

Thus by 1914 most pubs were in brewery possession, a situation whereby in the present context some 60,000 public houses are now in five large brewing company hands, the breweries opting for the off-licencing promotion of wine, spirits and beer, and varying types of on-licenced premises - wine bars, hotels, clubs, restaurants, discotheques - and serious provision of food.

The aim of the breweries seems to take on board the 1944 Morris Committee Report, summarised by the Errol Committee of 1972 in the trends since 1900, 'the brewing industry for most of this century has pursued a policy of "fewer but better". This has meant, in effect, a continuous process of closing down sub-standard houses while improving existing premises. This process has been reinforced by a number of factors. These include increased costs of distribution and changes in population major redevelopment schemes in most of the country's large cities. The effect has been a continued run down of public houses in rural areas, the closure of small public houses in a large number of towns and increasing concentration on larger outlets ... modernisation schemes which make this necessary are not, in our experience, always well received by established public house users'. (12) The apparently arbitrary nature of brewers' policy and the changes have not only resulted in a decline in numbers, but also the emergence of a somewhat 'middle-class' public drinking house. This is an important element of change. The attempt is not to penetrate brewing industry policy but some effort is made to determine how public- house participants view the change.

The next section examines drinking patterns in a little more detail, partly because there are important differences in the social appeal of different types of alcoholic drink, partly because drink and its consumption are still a central feature of public house activity, partly because in the contemporary situation both product promotion and consumption pattern merit attention.

Drink and Drinking Patterns

The pervasiveness of an alcohol-drink culture and prominence of the public house during the Victorian period, conceals a radical decline when examined in a longer-term perspective. As Harrison soberly observes: 'between 1831 and 1931 in England and Wales the number of on-licenses per head of population fell by two thirds, and in the UK the per capita consumption of spirits fell from 1.11 gallons to 0.22, and that of beer from 21.6 to 13.3 standard gallons'. (13)

The variety of usages of alcohol go far beyond its meaning in relation to the public house. The social dimensions of alcohol, the beliefs and occasions in which it is used, and the public house remain unexplained without an awareness of such dimensions. What may have happened is not a simple decline in drinking patterns paralleled alongside the decline of the public house. In fact neither may have declined since 1935, they may have changed their context with different outlets, and they may have broadened their range of alcoholic beverages, but it is doubtful if they have declined absolutely. An examination between 1935-197 l of policy in terms of licensing legislation reveals that off-licences increased from 22,115 to 27,733, a rise of over 25%. The number of licensed unregistered clubs increased from 15,982 to 27,733, an increase of over 80%. The numbers of restricted on-licences, although only introduced in 1961 (for restaurant and restaurant and pub combined) by 1975 had reached 14,694. The number of public houses shows a decrease from 75,062 to 64,614. The net effect in the post- 1935 situation has thus been an increase in licensed premises and a decrease in public houses - the total number of licensed premises has increased from 113,159 to 138,885 between 1935 and 1975.

It is interesting to speculate about the interpretation of such trends. Have the working class forsaken the public house for the working-class club? Can the public house be said to be colonised by the middle class? [s there any support for the privatisation of family and lifestyles of the working class? What evidence is there of that in terms of the newer styles of drinking where there are indications of the newer consumer groups - women and young people. Do these trends reveal anything about brewers' policy and licensing practice in relation to the public house in the wider spectrum of other kinds of contexts in which alcohol is consumed? Are we drinking more or less, more but differently? Have we a situation where the pub is declining but alcohol drinking is increasing? Does the fact that the brewers have taken the canned off-licenced trade with vigour reveal anything new - drinking in the home rather than the pub?

It is always somewhat easier to ask such questions than to answer them, particularly as we move towards the European scenario and enter the new millennium. There are some clues which will yield an answer to some of these questions, particularly as they are relevant to the changing nature of the public house. Such changes focus on the frequency of usage of different licensed contexts and social differences in alcohol consumed in relation to those contexts, thus 'just under a third of informants claimed to visit a public house once a week or more often, another 12% one to three times a month. After public houses, home is the most popular place for having a drink - 30% do so once a week or more often, another 12% do so a least once a month. A quarter of informants drink at a club at least once a month, but only 16% do so at a restaurant and 8% in a hotel .. .it would appear that nearly three quarters of the adult population visit a public house sometimes, and more than this (78%) have an alcoholic drink at home at least occasionally' . (14) The importance of such a comparative finding is not only to place the pub in a wider context, it also places the activity in a variety of situations. There are also some useful pointers to the social composition of pub users and types of alcoholic drinks consumed, both of which add to the evidence of considerable social changes when contrasted to the 1938 Mass Observation study and the social-class usage pinpointed by Harrison and Bailey in their historical analysis. It is worth reminding ourselves that statistical analysis does not reveal the meaning of the situation to the participants, however taking this into account, Bradley and Fenwick offer the quite remarkable findings that, 'when frequent pub goers are analysed by age, sex and class, it emerges that pub going is predominantly a male occupation .. and youthful one. Two thirds of the men (67%) come into the regular public house visiting category, compared with only a quarter (26%) of the women .. .if t he public houses are young and masculine in tone, they are almost entirely classless in general, if not in the case of particular establishments' . (15) What such data reveals is that change is occurring, albeit more than one sort of change. What can we tell about what is happening about alcohol drinkers, particularly those who go to the pub, the club or stay and drink at horne?

There are some differences which are note worthy; the semi-skilled and unskilled are moving to the clubs - more than twice as much in the North of England. At the same time the improved pub policy enforced by the licensing justices and approved by breweries - the reduction of public house density, open plan, carpeted bars, improved decor, the 'theme pub with the attraction of the new customers - of women and young people, may well indicate changes in terms of frequency of pub visiting. There may well be some working class going to clubs - where the drink is considerably cheaper and children are allowed in - and resistance to assimilation into middle-class lifestyles and patterns. Equally there may be some extension in the middle classes of original lifestyles in a horne from horne environment, a more 'frier, frier' environment than 'sawdust and perpendicular' drinking. So how much has the pub improved its image and customers' perceptions of the experience it provides?

Work in the Public House

The majority of public houses are not free but are owned by the large brewing companies which determine whether they are tenanted or managed, who is installed as tenant or manager, and closely control the outlet in terms of the product sold - alcoholic beverages being charged for at the brewer's rate. The tied-house system may take a number of forms: 'in the first, the brewery company owns the freehold or the leasehold of the property and the publican, or licensee, is a salaried manager, paid a fixed wage, possibly with a bonus by results .. not only do the goods he retails come from the brewery, but also his glasses and household goods ... a second kind of tie gives the publican greater nominal independence. He is a tenant of the brewery and pays a rent to it. The rent usually takes the form of a low flat payment for his accommodation and a variable 'wet rent' paid according to the number of barrels of beer he sells in the relevant time period ... there are even looser forms of tie, the publican may own the property and the tie may be based merely upon a loan or mortgage given by the brewer, granted to finance the purchase of the house or stock-intrade' . (16) The tie, in its different forms, thus binds the publican to the product of the brewery and the property of the brewer.

Apart from the range of economic criticisms of the tied-house relationship, Cooper indicates graphically according to a verse by the door to the gents, 'the publican stood at the golden gate, his head was bent and low, we meekly asked the man of fate, which way he had to go. What did you do St. Peter asked, to seek admission here? I kept a pub on earth, said he, for many and many a year. St. Peter opened wide the gates and beamed on him as well, come inside and choose your harp, you've had your share of hell '. Apart from the fact that a publican works 90 hours a week, just what is the relationship the publican has to his family, the various authorities to which he is responsible, the brewing authority and for the drink he serves? Each area has a different degree of freedom, different responsibilities. Part of the study here is concerned with such a role since it appears that the publican has a crucial part in shaping the context, the activities which occur, the drink consumed, the kind of pub which is also a family context. No aspect of public house is left untouched by drink - from customer behaviour, to drinking behind the bar, to drink-induced sociability as a dimension of social interaction. Attention now turns to the ways in which drink and drinking may shape the work dimensions of the publicans' role. The patterning is extremely complex, partly because such pervasiveness is so complete, partly because much activity and interaction, while not centred upon drink and drinking, would not be explicable if these were removed.

Perhaps the first and most obvious point is that the tie has the direct effect that anyone pub sells the company brands of beer. The brewers have agreed 'swap' arrangements, but even so the regular beer drinkers know which pubs sell 'their' pint. There has been a stage when brewers had the view that standardisation and the switch to lighter nationally market beer was best, thus, 'in the 1950's 40% of all draught beer was mild .. one pint in ten now drunk is keg, the beer which has some of the characteristics of draught and some of bottled beer and some drinkers say, the better points of neither .. maybe your beer is processed, chilled, filtered and pumped out of a tanker'. (17) Without indulging in the product standardisation debate there is no doubt that the highly successful campaign for real ale (CAMRA), and that for real pubs (CARP), have shown how much resistance there can be to the carbonated and pasteurised product.

A second way in which drink enters into the publican's work role is in the technology of work. Most of the technology is located near the bar and the most obvious signs of this are the beer pumps and optic-measured bottles. The introduction of beer machines which 'pour' the legal pint equates with the hand pumps which used to build the biceps if not profitability. Measured pints, legally required, no longer depend upon so much of the eye judgement of the server as on the reliability of a mechanised process. What the customer rarely sees is the cellar aspect of the same process - the stacked steel barrels and connected equipment which raises beer under pressure to the dispensing point in the bar. The mechanisation of the process might be romantically mourned but tapping barrels and retaining authenticity might be a customer, rather than a publican, view of the process, 'I had to learn to tap the barrels too ... when I started I found it easier to sit astride the barrel ... and bang it from above, until I leaned over too far and fell off .. .I quickly became a mass of bruises and gaping wounds. My thumbnails were blackened through being continually hit with a large wooden mallet ... and there were as many notches on my shins as there were on the butt of Davy Crockett's gun'. (18) In essence this takes place 'backstage'. The beer pipes have to be cleaned, crates of beer brought up from the cellar, delivery of beer received, ancillary sales items purchased and accounts kept all in the time outside of opening hours. Mechanisation of the actual beer measuring and dispensing process, although important, is only a small element in the total process. The publican does not lose in the process the total autonomy in deciding who to serve, when and how much.

The third important aspect linked to drink and drinking is the requirement imposed on the publican to 'maintain social order', in a context which has the potential for unconstrained behaviour - for dis-inhibition. There are numerous media accounts of 'pub violence', although it is difficult to separate what happens outside a public house from what happens inside. The recent moves to introduce a non-alcoholic hour extra at the normal end of a pub evening might introduce an element to reduce the effects of alcohol consumption. (19) The concept of 'violence' obscures the wide variation in normative behaviour but Marsh pinpoints this occurrence - based upon only when the police become involved in an assault or disturbance, thus: 'pubs on the whole are extremely safe places in which to spend your time. If you were to spend a couple of hours each day in a typically average pub, the probability is that you would see only one fight in about eight years .. .the real question is not why there is any violence at all in the pubs, but why some pubs are more violent than others'. Marsh distinguishes between 'low risk' and 'high risk' public houses, asserting that, 'violence is certainly more frequent in some types of pub. Inner-city pubs which cater for a predominantly young group of people and have only a few regular customers tend to have the highest rate. This isn't terribly surprising ... those which promote live pop-music or pool tables have particular problems   pubs which have managers tend to have more problems than those with tenants. This applies within both high-risk and low-risk categories. Similarly young inexperienced landlords are more likely to have more trouble than their older seasoned colleagues. These differences cannot be explained away be saying that the old hands are more likely to be given the nice middle-class pubs by the breweries. This is true, but we were careful to take this into account in analysing our material'. (20) It is worth examining some of the observations made by Marsh since he himself does not appear to realise the possible implications of the research findings, to judge from the way important issues are passed over. Why is it that some pub have 'more problems'? Is it because the publicans have a different relationship to customers, are some simply' doing a job' and sharing in the normative context? Why is it to be expected that violence is measured 'isn't terribly surprising' in pubs used by young people. Is it because there may not only be a higher level of casual usage, but something more important, the expectations of sexual rewards, male competitiveness and negotiative social space? There may be middle-class pubs but how are they used, a public situation of private interaction? The fact that violence occurs at all 'is not surprising' is a bland and un-lightening assertion. It says nothing about the process, social or bio-social, which takes place in the context itself. Finally the equation between violence and 'assaults and disturbances' might be better and more firmly located more in the range of behaviours of which it forms an integrated part.

The maintenance of social order within the pub constitutes a crucial part of the publican's role, and attention now turns to this, with particular attention to the publican themselves. Marsh himself pinpoints the proneness in the pathology of alcohol consumption by occupational role and the publican figures high in this list. The work aspect of the publican's role is complex and lends itself to the humorous claim that 'a publican must be a democrat, an autocrat, an acrobat, a doormat. He must be able to entertain prime ministers, pickpockets, pirates, philanthropists and police and be on both sides of the political fence, a footballer, golfer, bowler, tennis player, darts champion and pigeon fancier. He has to settle arguments and fights and he must be a qualified boxer, wrestler, weight lifter, sprinter and peacemaker .. to sum up: he must be outside, inside, offside, glorified, sanctified, crucified, stupefied, cross-eyed ... and if he is not the strong silent type there's always suicide'. (21)

As revealing perhaps is how the publican deals with a case of closing time, 'We soon discovered that getting the customers out of the bar by half-past ten was not only impossible, but also unheard of ... by dint of shouting above the hub-bub and pushing among them to collect the empty glasses, we just managed to get them out by 11 pm, only to be called up an hour later with a request for six cases of brown ale and the pianner please'. (22) The much echoed claim in the historical and biographical material that 'more than in any other business, success or failure depends almost entirely on the personality of the man [or woman] behind the bar' (23), is a recognition that a publicans' role is a fine balance between the work-leisure dynamic of the situation. How is social order sustained in a time-free yet a time-regulated context, in which sensual joys sometimes spill over into unconstrained behaviour, in which an earthy and sensuous culture stands in sharp contrast to the legal norms which regulate public behaviour. It is in this social context that the publican is a participant and yet a non-participant, part of an 'in group' and yet the central 'outsider' in the situation, a volunteer conscript in the relational nexus of sociability, drinking, games and everyday pub happenings. The work side and the social side to the openness of dis-inhibition, so that the process of participation and the range of tolerated behaviour may deepen and widen during the drinking process, thus creating licensed familiarity. We shall examine in more detail where the publican is located in this ambiguous and conflicting complex, particularly in relation to alcohol as a 'behavioural modifier [which] promotes the expression of a variety of shared and idiosyncratic values in the individual and a large measure of socially shared and communicable values ... diminishing social distance and strengthening group bonds' (24), which form important issues when regular public-house users are interviewed in the three pubs where this took place.

Conclusion

The rapidly changing brewery situation, with bigger and 'better' companies, the emergence ofthe tied house linking the pub and the publican, and the drink and drinking habits of our population, plus the sort of problems for the publican of exercising the role inherent with contradictions, have been the subjects covered by this chapter. We have yet to explore in depth the participants themselves, what they do in pubs, how they view some of the contradictions, and what they think of the changes. Thus we turn to what may be the most important section so far in our quest for this enigma.

Chapter 4 References

1. Harrison B., Drink and Society in England 1815-72: A Critical Bibliography pp204-205, in International Review of Social History, Vol XII, 1967, part 2

2. Harrison B., Drink and the Victorians, Faber and Faber, 1971

3. Data from the paper by Hawkins K. and Radcliffe R., ·Competition in the Brewing Industry', Bradford University Management Centre, 1970

4. Ibid p58

5. See Mathias P., The Entrepreneur in Brewing 1700-1830, in The Entreprenuer, papers presented at the 1957 Annual Conference of Economic History Society

6. The Times, 10thApril, 1827

7. Harrison B., op cit p60

8. Monkton H.A., A History of the English Public House, Bodley Head, 1969,p89

9. Ibid p92

10. Vaisey J., the Brewing Industry 1886-1951, an Economic Study for the Economic Research Council, Pitman, 1960

11. Ibid pp8-1O

12. Baxter J., The Organisation of the Brewing Industry, unpublished PhD thesis, University of London 1945, Table 58

13. Ibid, Harrison B., pp37-38

14. Bradley and Fenwick, Public Attitudes to Liquor Licensing Laws in Great Britain, OPCS, HMSO, London, 1874, pp2-8

15. Wilson G.B., Alcohol and the Nation, Nicholson and Watson, London,

1940

16. Hawkins K. and Radcliffe R, op cit pp24-37

17. Heaton v., Run Your Own Pub, Dent and Son, 1973, pp20-27

18. Reynolds M., Prisoner in the Bar, Phoenix House, 1958, pp 11 0-111

19. Last Orders' - fear for Country Pubs, the Guardian, 30 March 1999

20. Marsh P., Violence at the Pub, New Society, 12th June 1980

21. Reynolds M., Prisoner in the Bar, op cit p34

22. Ibid p34

23. Cooper D., The Beverage Report, pll0

24. Lemert E.M., Alcohol Values and Social Control, in Society, Culture and Drinking Patterns, p554

Chapter 5

The 'Respectable' Working-Class Public House

The pubs I include in my sample depended upon the objectives to be achieved and the detailed analysis undertaken. It was decided to take the typical 'respectable' working-class pub and a typical 'posh' middle-class pub and then draw conclusions. However in chatting to regulars in the first pub I became aware of a third type of 'rough' pub, one you visited and stood against the wall, to avoid a knife in your back, where you stood down the bottom end of the bar with the unemployed, where Dave was king and sat on the only available stool, where what was available was 'interesting literature' freely circulated, and where the publican was always out 'searching for a car', where the children were invariably present from early lunchtime through to six o'clock. Perhaps I enjoyed the challenge without too much fear about what could happen. So the 'rough' pub was included in the sample. The research framework was over two years and included an observational - participant approach initially, and then the interviewing of the regulars concerned - both women and men.

The historical framework thus far deployed has two dangers: firstly it reduces to single dimensions the highly complex changes which have occurred; and secondly the opposite danger of reifying the pub to an independent social content. These dangers have lead to a middle-range typological approach in the first chapter, very much concentrating upon the structural aspects and the social usage patterns of the pub. Then we examined the various dimensions, the historical, legal and social factors, not within an abstract framework but with a reflexive orientation, a generous 'grounded framework' approach. In this I hope we have avoided the dangers and placed the public house as a centre of the scattered and tantalising approach. To a large extent the framework has not sought patterns of organisation, usage and meaning; questions have been posed but not answered. So one turns to the findings of this study. Findings which are specific, only a small number of pubs were studied; findings which may not be universal but may be typical; findings which encapsulate the usage patterns, known meanings and behaviour diversity in the public house, thus 'we are open to two opposite temptations; firstly to press our conceptions as final, and to determine that the facts shall be squeezed into them, no matter how; and secondly, when candour compels us to give up this game, to throw over our conceptions altogether as vehicles of genuine truth ... we are wrong if we take the fragment for the whole; and equally wrong if we take it for a fragment of something other than reality. It is real but not the whole of reality'. (1)

The basic question now is the means used to work out the theoretical framework in our first chapter, a framework which offers a possible basis for an interpretation and understanding of the public house as social reality.

Approach to the Working-Class Pub

The public house is an intriguing place. Imagine you were a man from Mars or a women from Venus, what would you make of it? Not a lot maybe 'the most difficult things to study .. are the familiar, the stuff out of which our everyday experiences are constituted. These taken for granted occurrences and relationships are elusive and slippery, providing no vantage points .. no outline perspective or scaffolding on which to stand'. It was also apparent that the moment we step 'into the role of observer he becomes reflective about himself, about those he is interacting with, about those he is watching in interaction .. to the extent that he can raise questions about what occurs, he can also question how and why such events take place'. (2) However it also became apparent that viewing the familiar as 'unfamiliar' yielded some definable scaffolding and some curious taken-for-granted interaction could be uncovered in relation to the public house. It was also discovered that sustaining the role of 'observer' becomes increasingly difficult with the amount of alcohol consumed (very much as the Worktown study found after the ninth pub). The participant observer decided to drink pints of coke - a drink which looks remarkably like Guinness - dark, strong and 'a man's drink'. The concealment element in the situation was not entirely sustainable when others were 'treating', whilst the public nature of the bar situation meant that ordering one's own drink was itself an open act. In relation to the participation in a working-class pub, the variables constituting the structure of the situation were allowed to 'emerge' from the data, and develop the theoretical framework as a social context.

Public House Social Space

The first clear structural aspect which emerged in relation to the activities and behaviour of participants, was the 'space' which consisted in the area of public usage of the pub. The pub concerned divided itself into three distinct spatial areas: a bar area; a games area; and a dining or distinct sitting area. Carpet was in evidence everywhere, with plastic flowers and two wall clocks - both showing the incorrect time. The public house itself was small but' open plan' to the extent that much of every room could be 'seen' from the bar. The social division of physical space itself provided the definition of where things 'normally' occurred - at least at the typical beginning of opening time. The bar, the games area and the sitting and dining area, were all open to drinking activity - one could carry one's pint anywhere in the pub, and people did. One of the important but obvious aspects in terms of the social usage dimension was the fluidity of drinking usages of such areas - fluidity which was unvarying over any particular time period. The physical setting for activities and behaviour was very much part of the 'familiar' for the regular pub users - they saw that eating meals 'at the bar' for instance was not 'allowed', (except for the publican, who saw it very much as his perogative). Games could only be played in the games area if fixed equipment was used, thus the playing of pool was itself restricted to the games room. However, other games - cards and dominoes - were played in the dining area whether people were eating or not. Of particular interest was the activity and behaviour which occurred around the bar area since, although people could venture anywhere in the pub with their pints and their partners (except behind the bar and to the toilets), the bar was revealed as the most fluid of social areas in the public house. In some real sense it was the 'natural arena of social interaction'. It was the point to which customers converged to purchase their drinks, it was also the area of what Goffman termed 'unfocussed' interaction - people meeting and exchanging in a face-to-face situation various kinds of information and aspects of their 'selves'. The shape of the bar was L-shaped so it aided the process. The designated social usage of the space, to a large extent, derived from the physical structure of the setting, but the actual social usage related to several interdependent factors - whether people came by themselves or not, the focal interest of their visit and their' class'. The designated social usage did not correspond to the actual usage, it was found that this related to the dynamics of group formation and to variations in openness to 'face-to-face' encounters of users of the public house. From careful observation (clutching one's pint of 'Guinness ') it was concluded there were three social usages of the 'fixed space' in question.

Firstly there was distinctly public or OPEN SPACE - any topic of conversation could be initiated and carried on principally at the bar when typically people were detached from their friends or partners. It was also clear that often those sitting at the bar were 'open' to engagement. At the pub concerned it was the bar which formed the principal focus of interaction of a predominantly male, working-class, middle-aged group of 'regulars'. It was a situation of much private repartee - typically the repartee was sexual and personal. Interestingly, the publican himself was a major protagonist in the process, often sitting with customers on their side of the bar and eyeing newcomers with the expertise of a bullfighter, ready to impale the newcomer in an attempt to find out what was happening in their work life, sex life and personal relationships generally. Money, sex, sport, cars and wives - usually other people's were the major foci of discussion with the rapid switches of subjects and levels. It was a fascinating and lively discussion. During the summer - May to early October - since the pub was close to a caravan site we often had in the occasional non-regular who went away amused, angry or who was genuinely involved. Some were so involved that they stayed seated at the bar all night with a nucleus of others, but also there was an ebbing and flowing tide of regulars who came to the bar to buy their drinks and were either incorporated or excluded. Inclusion or exclusion strategies by the bar group were clearly to be observed - and the major mechanism of such strategies was the joke or terse comment or just a refusal to engage in conversation. The openness of the bar region was both structural and inter-actional. It was the area of situated activity which frequently was the focus of normative deregulation. Social conventions were frequently ignored or diluted; other men's wives and women alone, were hugged (never other wives husbands) thus infringing the public norm of 'minimum physical contact' in public places. Comments, jokes and 'freedom to engage', which would have been considered out of place in other situations - and even elsewhere in the pub itself - were accepted and practised and particularly on women who were alone at the bar - and they were quite rare.

A second cross-cutting social usage of the fixed space of the observed public house was distinctly NEGOTIABLE SPACE - areas of the public house which were clearly open to a fluid interaction, where the observer could be himself, and could join in a discussion or not, where there was a loosening of the bonds of 'mutuality', in the process of group formation and re-formation. Non-sitting areas of the pub appeared to offer the opportunity for casual encounter and interaction - but not to the same extent or on the same open terms as the bar area. People would cluster in standing groups and depending upon the focus of attention - the game in progress, the topic of discussion, the known-ness of a group member, the excitement of winning on the games machine - they would 'negotiate' themselves into and out of often topic- specific or exchange-specific encounters. Some people would 'drift around' the negotiable areas of the pub, looking for someone they knew, frequently with whom they had 'a deal' or particular purpose in meeting. The negotiable pub space was fascinating to observe - the pub observer felt he was in the 'beer sodden culture' of yesterday and had found that the 'pub was the shortest way out of the city' compared to any other route. There was a constant trickle of people to and from the bar, the games area and the toilets. Members of groups, in negotiable space, usually had no 'situational shields' with which to insulate themselves from other group members - they could not 'hide' behind their newspapers or pints, nor could they have immediate access to the publican as a mechanism for arbitration or a means of a final judgement. The absence of such shields could in some measure account for the fluidity of such groupings and their impermanence. Although such groups were mainly male, the male being the social partner to the group, there were some all-female groupings. It was noticeable that such female groups were never found at the bar. Equally, it became clear that women composing such groups had come in with a male partner who was elsewhere in the pub. Women rarely if ever came by themselves to form part of a grouping in the negotiable space.

The third dimension of social space found in the pub observed can be termed CLOSED SPACE. The public house offered clear areas of social usage where couples or people could be alone without the exposure or necessity of interaction. Such closed space was again fairly discernible from observation. The physical distribution of seating and tables made it possible for people to decide whether to remain in their personal sociability spheres and private social space, or indicate whether they were available for open engagement. The sorts of signals offered by people, and the sorts of shields used, clearly indicated whether people were available for engagement and interaction. Typically couples, who came into the public house, intent upon each other, could remain in their closed social space for as long a time as they wished. It was interesting that the success of excluding others was somewhat variable depending where the face-to-face open interaction was occurring. The games area in particular, although offering tables, chairs and bench-type seating was equally negotiable; it was relatively easy to 'open up' the games process and the mildly competitive participants around the pool table easily penetrated the closed social space of surrounding areas. The dining area was the most closed of the social space available since there was no 'through traffic' to the bar, the toilets or the games areas, people who wished to be alone could sit and eat and engage whatever they wished to engage in - certainly mild sexual behaviour was on the menu. The second area of most successful closed social space to judge by usage, was the area with bar stools and tables immediately opposite the main bar. One could 'retire' from the cut and thrust of negotiable space to the area for resting or weary travellers, or those having a private conversation over a meal.

The three categories of OPEN, NEGOTIABLE AND CLOSED, social space formed part of the scaffolding of the everyday events in the public house. Jokes were given, stories told, incidents related, life patterns explored, situations stimulated, men and women were levelled in their humanity, it was the 'stuff of which humanity was made'. So was this against the reasoned self or personalised self image? Was the public house a place to relax and let the relaxation of the self become more real? As the story unfolds, is it a gender basis of behaviour, which begins to inform the basis of action in this working class context? Is gender an issue which begins to change the scaffolding of social-space usage. It was certainly present, but tended to be cross cut by other social variables. The cross-cutting process was very much related to the time of day, particularly day or evening, the day of the week, either Friday or Saturday, but not invariably so. In the disjuncture of physical with social space there were distinctly other factors such as when the negotiable space was crowded with the spill-over from the bar area, and such crowding occurred particularly at weekends. However the most interesting change occurred under the impact of alcohol itself. It was alcohol that provided the passport to the individual for community membership, which shaped the basis for entry to the group, which meant they could be what they wanted to be, and be what they were as a social being - open to choice, persuaded that open, negotiable, or closed social space was our preference, or we may drift from one to the other gradually which alcohol implodes - occasionally dramatically - as though the norms of the bar gradually extended and as the public house filled up, the 'licensed familiarity', whereby all were available for encounters and interactions, become the dominant norm. The process was not consistently pervasive and to some extent dependent upon the degree to which those in closed and negotiable social space abdicated their position. Such abdication appeared to be related to pre-existing friendship patterns, or the extent to which people 'knew' each other, having previously met in the public house or elsewhere. It is important, thus, not to over emphasise the implosion - the 'licensed deregulation' - of social space under the impact of drinking alcohol, but it was clearly the case that the reduction in physical space with increasing numbers, also generation of a blurred separation of areas of social space, shields to social encounters become less effective, designated usages of physical space yielded to negotiable ~ocial interaction. The fact that noise and activity levels increased - the hubbub of voices, the volume of music, the flow of people to and from the bar, the games area and the toilets, and permitted behaviour of carrying one's drink anywhere in the public house, generated a physically contained yet socially distinct 'public or open social space experience'. Such an experience appeared a central cross-cutting dimension, linking the nature of social usage, the time framework of participation, and the patterns of social interaction of participants.

Some support for the observation experienced can be found in Cavan's description of Bar Encounters, 'Those present have the right to engage others, acquainted or not, in conversational interaction ... sociability is the most general rule in the public drinking place n' there are no protective goods, no newspapers, letter or books to serve as an alternative form of involvement n. physical bar structures form the centre of gravity, and it is here that the greatest amount of contact occurs between strangers in the premises. Thus one solution to the problem of setting oneself apart from the sociability of the establishment is to avoid the bar and sit at the tables'. Cavan's analysis is located in the United States which varies in key respects to the United Kingdom (e.g. you cannot carry your drink around with you). However in terms of Encounters the claim about 'the bar' is the evidence of an open area where you may meet people. (3) She does not make the claim made here about types of social space, the separation of physical structure from such social space usage, and the way in which alcohol affects the regulars in terms of their social interactions. We now turn to the second issue which examines the social relations and sexual interaction in the public house of respectable working-class complexity.

Social Relationships and Sexual Interaction

In taking in social relationships their linkage to sexual interaction is a key decision, taken in the observational process. Who met whom, why, and what they did and the social relationships within the working-class pub cannot easily be separated from the non-public house relational networks. They are contingent, but since the question we are seeking an answer to lies in the pattern of interaction within the public house, it will be interesting to adopt the questions as set and see where they lead, what difficulties they pose, if they have any conundrums, if the respectable working-class public house is at discernible from the objective data. At best the evidence is fragmentary and precarious but at least we will not be left with 'statistics without meaning', as has happened before in relation to the pub. The findings on class sociability patterns, and the ambivalence posed for unaccompanied women, were of special interest. Also some note seems to be raised by Clough of a danger of 'naive voluntarism' , in her own words, 'The contemporary approach to public behaviour has limited the possibilities of using ethnographies of situated activity from investigating the manifestations of status differentiation ... this is because approaches to situated activity which emphasise interpersonal reaction are often critical of conventional variable analysis, in that categories such as class and status, are viewed as variables independant of the act of the definition of them. But carried to extreme, an interactionist position can be equivalent to a naive voluntarism but not with the effect of ignoring the potential meaning of the situation to the participants of the public house. The structuring of social relationships within the working-class pub observed are best described through the particular categories and what they did. Some account of 'why' can then be explored.

The first clear factor was the proportion of 'regulars , to 'casuals' in the public house. Some 80% of customers were regulars and they came once a week or more often. Although it took some time to establish which users of the pub were regulars, it was concluded that the vast proportion did live locally. The majority of regulars - and most casuals - were manual workers. Lorry drivers, motor mechanics, joiners, labourers and factory workers, but also there was a number of middle class, including a foreman, a college lecturer, two teachers and a company director - the last living just three miles from the pub. Few of the manual workers worked in the same place although they knew each others work and place of work. The majority of regulars were men, although over the period which lasted two years it was estimated that 20% of regulars were women - women accompanied by male escorts, particularly on Friday and Saturday evenings.

In the period of observation certain patterns emerged in terms of the relationship between regulars. There was a clear group of bar regulars (all male) who rarely did anything more than sit at the bar and drink pints - and they were all around middle age, in various degrees of marital disintegration. They never ventured into the closed or negotiable areas of the pub - except under duress - and appeared to be key informants of the publican to keep him updated on 'what's happening' and provide unpaid advice, and 'bargain offers' - cheap tyres, loads of Tarmac, cheap vegetables, meat and timber, plus some clearly questionable bargains in terms of rings, watches and various consumer durables. Venturing to the bar at certain times could have the effect of watching the publican and a regular 'disappear' clutching items in a black plastic bag. Usually they were innocuous bargains, but sometimes not.

The group of bar regulars were all 'working class' and if one of the middle class participants appeared at particular times, he was challenged fairly quickly to a game of pool- thus removing him from the situation. Alternatively, the publican would retreat to a corner - without comment from the bar group. The 'maleness' of the group and the fact that it regularly convened between 4 and 8pm most evenings was not itself such a surprising discovery. What was interesting was the close bonds they formed with each other and with the publican. None was ever refused a drink after hours, even though they may have walked the half mile there and back to the next public house, and reappeared after the legal hours of serving. It was as though having established the right to be served earlier it was regarded as a perpetuated right for the night. Few middle class stayed at the bar, if they came in before 8pm they retreated into the closed social space. The only exception to this pattern was the regular managing director. He was accepted because he was 'a self-made man', and seemed to use the group as a therapy session to explain the toughness of the decisions he had to make and the reasons why his marriage was in the process of disintegration - and we all wanted to know the real and unvarnished reasons for both.

The bar group was distinctly male, between 25 to 45 in age grouping, working class and never accompanied by wives, mistresses or female companions. They all lived locally, within a one to three mile distance ofthe public house. They shared the same class but there were lateral status differences arising from work expertise or job skills. It was very much an in-group and displayed noticeable interest, yet social distance, when the occasional middle class (to judge by dress, speech and car) appeared - and disappeared. Women were a fairly constant topic of conversation, either in terms of sharp lewd jokes or in terms of group members disclaiming that they were 'there' when partners 'phoned. The much discussed cost of sexual encounters, the casual way in which the women were regarded as sexual objects, the commiseration with the married men whose wives' hadn't been trained', was enough to convince the writer of this book about the primacy of said differences in working-class public-house culture. The public house was a place where women were taken apart, analysed and dissected as lovers, as working partners, family cooks, holders and spenders of money - the masculinity was evident. It was based upon the assumption that women just existed in order to please men and that if they had difficulty in any situation, women must be to blame - and the justifiable casual responsibility for that blame. Many of the men had partners, girlfriends, lovers, mistresses, or lived alone and different opinions depending who was in and what the latest problem was. The implicit judgement of not talking about religion or politics in the pub, gave the third topic, sex a more than even chance. If anything it was the 'hidden agenda' which kept the pub bubbling along. It also was a situation of alcohol immediacy, the lively cut and thrust of discussion, the familiarity of the participants to each other, the certainty of being a matured male. The masculinity and immediacy of the culture is a subject we shall return to. Let it be said that it is unwise to claim too much about one group, in one working-class pub, but the observations are offered as typical of the bar group, its masculine and bar-group culture. As I said earlier, this is a subject we shall return to.

The second distinct group of public-house users were young working-class men and women - in various states of relationship. The proportion of under 25 's who were regulars was a distinct nucleus - some 30% of the total of 80% - who formed an important separate group. Most of the younger group came as couples, at least in twosomes. They often did not stay together- the men teaming up with mates and the 'girls' sitting, watching and talking usually the males played pool or 'drifted around' the negotiable space and the bar area in search of 'somebody about something'. Occasionally a young couple would retreat into the closed social space - usually the dining area which was not visible from the bar and out of the flow of interaction, and would proceed with protracted physical- obviously sexual- contact which was more than just holding hands.

The usual time appearance of the group of 'young regulars' was 8 to 8.30pm and they tended to arrive by car - the approximate time the publican's wife appeared. Her arrival signalled the ending of the all-male bar group until about 10pm The male youths with their women were predominantly manual workers. They were the main patrons of the pool table, the juke box and the gaming machine. None were married although some had a rather married look about them. A great deal of interaction occurred in this group, however it was asymmetrical in character. Young women would almost never order their own drinks and they did not approach the bar. Also they saw the occasion as an equivalent of being 'taken out', and although they worked they let the men pay. Although the women were free to go anywhere in the pub they rarely did so. Much of the activity centred around the 'games element' in the situation. The women were usually inferior pool players who rarely played with the 'boys ' (except in a catchment situation)', if they played at all it was usually with another woman. Much of the process of initiating activity and decision taking seemed to be undertaken by the male - whether it was in buying drinks, deciding on the use of various machines, or even when to leave the pub. It seemed somehow as though the women were playing a role, that if they wanted to they could say no, or yes but I will discuss this with you when you are sober. The ease of the decision process should be regarded with some caution. It was true that from observation the young women appeared to be compliant, whether or not they were must remain an open question at this stage.

Usually the nucleus of young regulars gradually occupied the pool area, then the negotiable area of space, effectively translating the games area into their own open space - everyone was welcome. The sexual dynamics of the situation were difficult to interpret - as Merton once astutely observed, it is difficult to be everywhere at the same time - it was a sexually closed group but less of a socially-determined one. It was as if the 'vitality within fatalism' argument had yet to close. There were clear attempts by the young men to impress the women, as though masculinity had to be demonstrated and social virility was measured by male decision taking. There was little or no competitive drinking in the group.

Also rarely, if ever, were unattached women found in the group, they did not come into the pub on their own and even when they came in pairs they tended to sit together and be quite distinct by occupying their own closed social space. In observation and comparison with the bar group, the young regulars lived over a much wider geographical area and invariably did not walk to the pub. Also there was a distinct difference in the relationship with the publican - they tended not to be confidants and rarely engaged in the range of bar interactions.

The third distinct group of 'regulars' in the public house, were middle class in consumption and work terms, and usually between the ages of35 to 55. They drove quite expensive cars and usually appeared in the pub on their 'way out' (between 7 and 8pm) for the evening, or for a late evening drink (between 10 and l0.45pm) and almost without exception were accompanied by male or female companions. They almost also without exception established and maintained a closed social space - opposite the bar area and in the dining area. The general pattern of usage of this 'respectable working-class' public house was quite different from the other two groups identified. There was no participation in the pool game and no use of the juke box or gaming machine. Neither did the middle-class users sit at the bar - even when the bar was unoccupied. It was the middle-class users who frequently appeared with 'friends' who were staying for the weekend, or in a group of four on the way out, or on the way back, from dining out. There appeared to be strong middleclass norms of private interaction and they used the most physical shields the tables - to reinforce the privateness of their interaction with partners. Often 'working -class' couples in the same general age grouping would sit side-by-side, but almost without exception, middle-class couples would sit facing each other , in a very clear posture of private interaction in closed social space. The regular middle-class users thus usually sat, talked between themselves, drank perhaps two pints of beer (halves of larger or spirits in the case of women), took part in none of the public house activities other than drinking, and usually departed between 10.30 and 11 pm. Without interviewing these participants it was decided that the analysis could not be taken further, thus interviewing was decided, partly because of the intriguing results apparent from the working-class groups, and secondly the less than successful approach in understanding the middle-class group.

Something should be said about the lunchtime (12 - 5pm) session, which was used in a somewhat different way to the evening session in the working class -public house. One important difference was in the range of female groups that used the public house at lunchtime. Such groups tended to be composed of women factory workers, all drawn from the same workplace and most numerous on a Friday. Married women and co-habitees composed the majority of such groups. They tended to occupy the whole of the dining area and the area opposite the bar. They did not occupy the bar or the games area and formed a distinct caucus. They rarely ventured beyond their own group and seemed to find the public house a useful place for a quick, cheap lunch and each drank rarely more than two halves oflager. There was very little interaction between the female members of the several groups, and the casual users who frequented the negotiable areas and the bar. Casual users were a much higher proportion of total users at lunchtime and what became clearer was that there was a much more heterogeneous composition during that time. There were far fewer couples, a predominance of young to middle-aged males, and a much higher proportion of casual male users. There was a difference between working-class and middle-class male users of the pub between 12 noon and 5pm. Apart from how they looked, the former remaining at the bar in the pool area, the latter using the closed space and the negotiable area. There seemed to be a much faster turnover of customers, people checking their watches, being prepared to return to work, going on to another pub or meeting somebody, or even going to pick up the children from school. The publican himself tended to be irregular in his early afternoon appearances and, possibly because he was recovering from the night before, usually emerged to check the bar stock shortly before opening time, only to disappear and leave much of the serving to his wife and a part-time woman assistant.

Chapter Five References

I.   Hobhouse L.T., The Theory of Knowledge, Meuthen, 1896, p559

2.   Birenbaum A. and Sagrin E., People in Places: The Sociology of the Familiar, Nelson, 1973, p3

3.   Cavan S., Bar Sociability, op cit pp143-146

4.   Clough P.T., Sociability and Public Behaviour in a mid-sized City, in Studies in Symbolic Interactionism Vol 2, Jai Press, 1979 p361

Chapter 6

The Life of the Publican

The way a pub is, and operates, depends very much upon the publican. So far in our book this is generally what has been anticipated. He has the arrangement with the brewer, with the public and with the local magistrates to operate a 'good house'. The publican has lurked behind many of the situations and occasions we have identified, but has the situation changed that much? In the details which follow, what hope have we of understanding the ups and downs of the publican's role - his lifestyle, since he lives where he works, and works where he lives? What techniques does he use to maintain control, what use does he make of any particular group, does he have formal and informal strategies, how does he socially fit the family into the pub? How does he manage and control the consumption of alcohol in a relatively free context? These are the type of questions that it makes sense to ask. We should ask them if only in terms of the simple strategies of finding some answers. What seems appropriate is to carry forward the approach already adopted, namely an observational lurking in the pub selected, the Nelson, with these inherent questions, as they relate to the publican himself, in mind.

The two areas which seem crucial to the publican are as follows: firstly how does he relate to the customer, and control the pub situation with a variety of strategies; and secondly how does he shape his family with all the tensions and conflicts this might bring. The basic questions of how much of a profit he made and is it a career perspective, these type of questions were 'secondary' to the basic perspective of what he does in the job, and can he keep his family together. The publican was a tenant, not a manager, and among the regulars he had a reputation of being 'tough' and quite 'a drinker'. He was in his forties and living with his second partner, and there were six children - one in his teens. He had previously been a milkman before a publican.

The Publican and the Customer

Usually the publican was the first person to see the customer. Because of the position of the bar in relation to the door, the first encounter was for the customer to walk towards the bar. The nature of such an interface was almost sufficient to determine whether the customer was a 'regular' or not. Some drinkers were so regular in their drinking habits that their drink was almost standing on the bar even before they came through the door. To a large extent the process of serving was not so much a matter of dispensing the drink itself (he served a good pint), but the social interaction which accompanied it. The extent to which a customer was known provided the basis for familiarity of the usually brief encounter. The publican in such an interaction situation would adopt one of two strategies, either a 'humorous' strategy or an 'information' strategy. The humourous strategy was generally applied to the male middle class regulars, 'I see she's let you out then', or 'has she run away yet', 'Didn't think you could come out for a pint'. The information strategy was generally applied to working class male regulars, referring to a 'previous deal' or the possibility of 'free advice' on a new deal, or some enquiry about what has happened to 'so and so'. The brief interaction resulted in the firm establishment between the publican and his regular customers. It was a distancing and integrating process' carried out as a part of an open and public performance, and enabled the publican to both hold the interest and consensus of the regular bar group and also separate himself from the middle-class participants.

The publican himself had a distinct separate physical area in the pub - behind the bar - and depending upon 'who was in' and 'how busy he was serving' and whether the family were 'helping out'. He himself ventured out from behind the bar, often combining the collection of empty glasses whilst sitting and chatting with customers. The publican by right could approach any physical area of the public house and thus invade the different kinds of social space. The extent to which he did so was interesting in that it revealed something about the role-style of the publican himself. The publican concerned was most often found in the bar group, often forming one of the nucleus of the group between 8 and l0pm He rarely lingered in the negotiable space, and if not at the bar, could be found in the games area, often by his presence turning it into a negotiable or open interaction situation. The publican was a renowned pool player himself and when not playing, clearly commented on the standard of others. From observation it was clear that the publican least invaded the closed social space - couples at tables.

The observations reported above are interesting. The publican was firmly wedded to his 'role'. He was able to develop a role-style which enabled him to differentially relate to the dominant groups using the pub. In relation to the youth group there was evinced a grudging respect for the publican's own games skill and his 'tough masculine image', perhaps helped by being twice married, having an attractive wife some twenty years younger than himself, six known children and the reputation for being a 'stud'. To the bar group, mostly working class, middle aged and all male, the tough masculinity stance was reinforced by the publican's own views about women. A large calendar showing a new nude every month hung behind the, bar. The ways in which the publican jested about wives 'who had not been trained', and his frequent insulation of married members of the bar group, when their wives phoned ~ 'No, he hasn't been in', or 'He's just left' whilst nodding knowledgeably to the regular concerned - made clear his identification with the often~pressed view of the bar group, 'women are only good for one thing'. Such overt sexual stereotyping was a common norm in the cohesiveness of the bar group itself, whilst there seemed to be a 'trade off' in terms of insulation of 'male bar~ group members from their women, and the information and favours of the publican. The publican never handed out free drinks and was a drinking member of the group, and his own work experience - factory worker, labourer, milkman - meant that he had little to offer in particular work-skill terms and knowledge, but had a general empathy with the work situation of.members of the bar group itself. He did facilitate much information exchange and a blackmarket economy between group members, and the stereotyping of .women in overt sexual terms and the insulation of bar-group members from :'their' women, seemed an important part of the economic information exchange relationship between the publican and the members of the bar group.

In terms of the publican and the third group, middle-class couples, there was a much more segmented and circumspect pattern of behaviour. Most of the middle-class couples, as already pointed out, did not participate in the games side of the pub, neither did they participate in the bar group. The non-participation of the middle-class couples in the open and negotiable physical space of the pub offered the publican little scope for interaction except at the point of the purchase of drink itself. The publican himself appeared quite content to serve drinks, develop social distancing strategies in terms of joking relationships and to leave the couples to themselves. '

It seems somewhat futile to assume a mono-casual influence from the publican to his customer groupings. It was very much a process of reciprocity of social elements, an interdependence of age, sex and class of users, and the ways in which the publican articulated to the customer - work dimensions of his role. Some interesting aspects of the pub situation remain unreported, two are worthwhile pinpointing in terms of the publican - customer relationship. There were many others but these two will suffice to illustrate the dynamics of the situation.

As one involved in observational lurking, at this stage not talking to anyone about the analysis, I was intrigued by what I thought was a genuine discovery. The management by a publican of a public house - working class. I might be right or I might find that the factors were not typical, but above all I was probing the difficult fabric, so much an enigma in contemporary society. And I was starting at the beginning, in the face of all the factors which were historical and popular, rarely objectional and never contemporary.

Control Strategies

From observation the publican at the Nelson seemed to involve three key control strategies, and we need to look at these in some depth in the publican! customer relation sessions.

The first was positional control- the publican knew who came into his pub. The publican could see the entrance door from the bar. Certain customers, some of the bar group, were known for their alcohol consumption and toughness. The publican, as will be remembered, ate his dinner at the bar. He positioned himself with an eye on the door, either at one end or the other of the bar, so he could see any newcomer. His right was not only an indication of his status but also of his long experience (twelve years) at the pub concerned. Also reinforcing this strategy was the device operating the front door. It had a double inner entrance door system so that, wherever one was in the pub, in spite of it becoming very busy, one could hear 'the door', a fact that the publican did not devise but took advantage of whether he was collecting the glasses, or just chatting to someone.

A second control strategy was 'informal' and conversational or gestural in form. The publican had the legal right to refuse to serve any customers and could ask them to leave the public house without an explanation. This was not a much deployed strategy. Instead the publican deployed a range of informal strategies. At the most extreme he would ignore a customer altogether. Purchasing a drink at the bar was very much a matter of 'catching the eye' of the server. The people that the publican did not want in his pub, he tended to delay serving, and in one case ignored them completely. The success of this strategy was most clear in several cases observed, including some of the underage drinkers and on two occasions women by themselves. A more confrontational strategy was adopted in the cases of 'known troublemakers'. These were usually served with one drink and warned that any mis-behaviour would result in them being barred. The brief exchange was occasionally explosive. In one case a full pint of beer was smashed on the bar and it was a matter of fine timing whether the publican reached the other side of the bar before the man reached the outer door. On another occasion the publican was knocked down in 'negotiable space', and with the help of two regulars laid the offender out cold, depositing him none too gently at the side of the road.

The third strategy of control used by the publican was a formal one, that of barring someone. This, as indicated, was a rare event. None of the regulars wanted to be barred or to be known for being barred, it was a 'put down' process in a free leisure context and implied somehow that you had 'lost control' in what could be construed an open situation. The barring process occurred when two regulars, on different occasions, caused personal offence to other customers. One was barred for 'not having a bath for months' i.e. he smelt, and also he was too interested in a couple sitting in their own private space. The other regular was barred for dancing on the pool table at 1.30 in the morning. Dancing on the bar on another occasion late at night, and stripping down to his underclothes, was not treated in the same way, perhaps because the customer the next morning pinned up a note in the bar area apologising for his lax behaviour. The barring of a regular was on a short-term basis. It was rather like a democratic sin bin, the offender served his penalty and then the regular was allowed to return.

The positional~ informal and formal control strategies certainly varied with the time of evening and the amount of alcohol consumed by the publican himself. The positional strategy was used when the pub was not too full, most of the week and early evening. After 8pm particularly on Friday and Saturday, saw the operation of the informal control mechanisms, and these were in full operation by 10 pm. Both of the regulars, formally barred, were formally sanctioned late on Friday evening. The publican himself drank lager - a high alcohol content light beer - and after three or four pints was more inclined to resort to the informal sanction, particularly as the regulars of early evening bar group began to return about 10pm. The publican tended to close the pub when the number present was less than six, on one occasion on a Saturday evening/Sunday morning at 2.30am. He had been twice prosecuted in the twelve months prior to my analysis for serving drinks after hours, but considered himself unlucky. On one occasion attributing prosecution to serving of a casual drink by a member of the bar staff in his absence, on another the over zealousness of a new police officer. The pub itself had a supper licence extension - drinks could be served up to 12 midnight with meals. Only about 25% who stayed 'after hours' had meals. By 11 pm on a Friday and Saturday the regular bar group was in full spate, the games area busy, tables opposite the bar empty, the dining area and negotiable space full.

One interesting fact was that the publican himself appeared not that much concerned about the legal sanctions attached to serving alcohol well after closing hours. He imposed few sanctions on his regular customers, and himself had abandoned the semblance of role distance and become a full participant in the situation. In an informal chat with the writer of this book about serving drinks after hours and how he dealt with violence, he made it clear that most violence, in his experience, resulted from turning people out at 11 pm, 'People tend to go when they've had enough', and as for his pub, 'I run a respectable pub and we have no trouble here', were his comments. He drew a sharp distinction between the 'rough pub' and his own, the former being one where prostitutes were readily available, brawls a regular occurrence, a hundred people barred monthly and excessive drinking the 'norm'. The comment made me even more intrigued by such a pub. His own attitude of a relaxed approach to closing time and running a pub where there was 'no trouble', formed part of an assessment of the police tolerance of informal drinking after hours. On at least three occasions a police car parked outside the pub, after closing time, and drove away after about half an hour. The pub doors remained open and the substance of the publican's view appeared vindicated.

Apart from the control strategies of the publican to groups of customers, his observed behaviour in relation to women customers in particular deserves comment. Women were often the main focus of interest, partly stimulated by the publican's attractive wife, and particularly a topic for discussion among the members of the bar group. Women were viewed very much as the 'hunted' and men as the 'hunters' in the gender spectrum - with all that implies according to the publican. Women alone rarely came into the pub although there were some exceptions. The absence of women at the bar meant they could be talked about, jokes easily exchanged, stories told, situations quickly becoming the nexus of a working-class oral tradition of masculine 'facts'. It led through to a penetration of such a process, so successful that the author began to rethink what was going on. Was the basic division in fact that of gender, that women and men had different priorities and ways of viewing themselves and their field of personal choice, was it this which was beginning to unfold? Whatever it was, it seemed that the issue of women in the pub.

The publican regarded women as necessary to his public house custom and would readily leave the bar - collecting glasses - to chat to them. The degree of licensed familiarity was considerable, particularly through attempts to involve the male bar group in the private space which was opposite the bar. Young and physically attractive women, in couples, did come into the public house, sometimes waiting for their boyfriends. If they were unknown to the publican he would 'check them out'. The sort of strategy was 'Have you come from far ... are you meeting any of the lads ... have you met Fred over there, he's having trouble with his wife - how about him ... why don't you drink a real drink?' , and then, depending upon the sort of response, and which groups of customers were in the public house, tell a slightly blue joke or move back towards the bar. He never carried his drink with him on these occasions and showed little interest in the older women who also occasionally came in couples on the quieter days of the week. It could be that the publican wanted to check on their age, or he viewed the young women as notionally available - which seemed most likely from his comments

The strategy of the publican with unaccompanied women depended upon whether they were known by him to be attached or not. Sometimes married women would come in alone, the husband being a regular but 'working away', and sit at the bar or stand chatting to the other women they knew. Such women rarely came in before 8pm and usually left by IOpm, and it was about 8pm that the publican's wife joined him at the bar. Sitting at the bar alone, was a somewhat unusual happening for a woman, but acceptable if the wife's husband was himself a regular - and with one persistent woman, if he was not. The persistent and unattached woman is worthy of note since the publican quickly formed an opinion that she was 'out to pick someone up'. She was a nurse, drove her own car, was twenty years old, and almost always sat at the junction of the bar opposite the calendar of nudes. That the publican tolerated her at the bar and did not exercise exclusion strategies, nor did the rest of the regulars, maybe because she gave them free medical advice and because of the fund of 'horror' stories about the local hospital. She was certainly 'picked up' and regarded as 'easy' by the bar group members. The publican himself, when his wife joined him, usually went and sat next to her on the customer side of the bar, to learn more of her turgid emotional life, gain information on some medical condition - usually his own, a regular's or a relative's - and swap blue jokes. Having a woman as a bar regular was accepted by the publican, but suddenly she stopped coming to the pub, and it was understood that she had 'settled in with some fella and got herself sorted out'.

The Publican and Family Relationships

The pub was a tenanted one and in it lived, apart from the publican, his wife, and three children by his second marriage. To a large extent one could not penetrate or encompass the totality of family relationships of the publican, just those aspects which impinged on the public house - another side pursuit which we could easily jump to would be the family issue here. I report that which I observed, nothing more and nothing less, and then go on to offer a critical empirical assessment of a crucial role.

The publican's wife did not have any paid employment and helped with the bar at fixed times, lunchtimes and from 8pm at night. The youngish wife was popular and 'good fun' , yet revealed considerable conflict in relation to her role of running the pub. The children were theoretically banned from the bar after 8 pm at night but it rarely occurred that way, being a constant source of distraction and often expressed conflict. The obvious nature of conflict between family requirements. The publican often had overt hostility expressed by his wife when she appeared at the bar, since he regarded her as having major responsibility for running the home - literally upstairs. The wife's success in doing so was somewhat precarious. On one occasion I was invited upstairs to look at the television which was not working. The amount of chaos upstairs was evident with children's clothes, dirty crockery, items of children's play, in fact it was all in sharp contrast with the neatness of the pub downstairs. The music from the jukebox clearly penetrated the domestic living space and the demands of the family - getting the children to school, shopping, domestic work (e.g. washing, cleaning and meals), and the children going to various friends and voluntary organisations, imposed a great deal of physical strain upon her. I was sharply reminded that she rarely got to bed before midnight, 'it drives me bloody barmy' were her words, as I attempted to mend the television. There were clear signs of time-usage conflict as well as the noise and activity from the work side to the family side of the pub. The publican and his wife had frequent rows at the bar when she was late down or he sat 'doing nothing', which concluded with her being 'put in her place' by the publican, after her threatening to leave the 'bloody place, kids and all'.

It may be that the personal conflict and domestic chaos witnessed was by no means typical or usual, but it makes me suspect the bold claim that 'the happiest public house is often where the publican's family assist him in the place of paid staff' . (1) It could be that the conflict and strain observed in the publican! wife relationship derived from this being a second marriage for the publican. The fact that his first wife had left him shortly after his taking on the pub suggests that the combination of a family/work situation, the intra-penetration by 'work' of family life, and the problems these posed for the domestic division of labour, may make for particular problems. This is confirmed by the recent disappearance of the publican's wife - she had run off with one of the regulars who had 'taken a fancy to her'. As one publican's wife autobiographically observed, 'Spending the entire morning tethered to the bar was exclusive agony to me .. .1 was a complete captive from 11am to 2.30pm and after a week of Mrs Parson's piles, and Daisy's ulcers, and suspicious irregularity of Ada's daughter's periods, began to feel that I might make more money by opening a clinic .. .1 began to have a nagging suspicion there must be better ways of earning a living. Unfortunately I could only think of one and I felt a bit too old to stand the competition. I suddenly began to feel bored to screaming pitch'. (2)

The lack of free time together for the publican and his wife in the working public house was very clear. They virtually had no free time with each other as individuals. Also very clear were the very long hours worked - ninety hours a week suggested the publican - and worked at times which made the 'normal' family life almost impossible. When the demands of the family were added to the demands of working behind the bar, it does not seem surprising that the dissolution of the male group of regulars coincided with the not infrequently stormy arrival of the publican's wife - usually coping with a family disaster elsewhere, a child who had not come home, children fighting, or not being able to find pyjamas, or some other variant on the family crises. It is no wonder that the second wife also eventually 'went off' - in more than one sense of the term.

What conclusions can we draw from this tentative observational assessment of the publican, and his wife and family? The simple conclusion is perhaps that they should never had been married, but to phrase the answer in the sense of each enjoying a full and happy life, running a pub together, when the pub was an all pervasive way of life, offered a small chance of success. It was this pervasiveness which was time related, activity related and relationally related.

Long work hours, themselves exhausting, made family time precious and precarious. Husband and wife were rarely able to go out together, and when they were downstairs in the pub, time itself was a public experience. Friends tended to be pub patrons, whilst meeting' other' people was almost impossible since they were at leisure just when the publican and his wife were at work. This was particularly so since they worked and lived in the same place. It was also likely since the publican absorbed himself into the social norms of the dominant group of male users - thus directly implementing the brewers and local licensing justices requirement, to take care when and who is served with alcohol- however, it would have helped the publican had he not used this as a reference group. The notion of work autonomy may turn out true of external agencies, but is profoundly circumscribed by that merging of the daily organisation of domestic life, which circumscribe the interests and activities of married partners, particularly the time, activity and relational elements of the work demands of the respectable working-class public house.

Was it a working-class public house? In several senses it was, in the area of mixed housing, a terraced and pre-war housing estate and predominantly used by manual workers. The inside reflected the outside, with the many 'workers' forming patterns of interaction much more collective than individual in orientation. The collective class pattern was focused around the male bar group in a private situation of public interaction. The middle class were few and noticeable, individualistic interaction in a public situation, sitting and chatting with a partner in a closed social space. What of the women, women who seemed simply an appendage to men's activities, giving men the pro-active role, women the reactive or recipient role. Was this fair or equitable, is certainly based on close scrutiny of the sorts of ' ups and down' the publican experienced with his work and with his family. The role of women in pubs is almost a separate issue but we will return to the part they play and the difficulty of defining their role in both the posh, middle class and the rough, underclass pub, and how they define themselves in terms of their convictions, fears and triumphs - the dilemmas and conflicts they face. These conflicts emerge as alcohol seeps into the formal norms which govern behaviour and change the relationship, typically defined in the following way. 'Those women who venture into pubs, especially at weekends, can expect short shrift. Our barmaid asked one man why he never said please or thank you, and was told he had never said it to a woman yet and wasn't going to start now. Then came the flasher. A supposedly respectable middle-class man ... when she had locked the front door from the inside, he emerged from the gents, exposed himself, then pinned her against the bar trying to put his hand up her skirt. Large as life he rolled up the next day. Well I'd been swilling hadn't I, he said as I threw him out .. .if girls went into bars they got what they deserved, as for barmaids well that's what they were there for wasn't it? (3) We find that this starts in class but maybe it completes itself in sexual fantasy. There is a class basis, as Allan suggests, the difference lies in the sociability patterns of each group. The working class tended to have relationships which were more locality and situational specific, which tended to affirm the 'primacy of the interactional setting in which relationships developed for the working class'. For the middle class Allan suggests they define the' activity they undertook with their friends as secondary to the reality of friendship'. He claims the relationship is more important than the context, the middle-class couples in their closed social space contrasts with the working-class group with their mates whom they met in the pub, telling jokes and stories. How far is it then that class-based differences in terms of patterns of male sociability lead to expressed sexual differences in terms of behaviour? Or is it a question of different methods but to the same objective - the contrast between middle and working class is considerable at one level, but is it so, particularly with the respectable working-class public house in mind. We now turn to an analysis of the 'middle class' and the 'rough' pubs for further clarification of the role of the public drinking house in contemporary society.

Chapter 6 References

1. Rowntree B.S. and Lavers G.R., English Life and Leisure, Longman, Green and Co., 1951,p176

2. Reynolds M., Prisoner in the Bar, Phoenix House, 1958, pp97-8

3. The Guardian, 8th June 1979, p9

Chapter 7

The 'Posh' Middle Class Public House

The taking on of a second pub, middle class, was to a large extent in the context of the framework already worked through. Nothing however was certain. How did I know before entering the pub that it was middleclass? The first pub had been small, local, in the middle of mixed houses and flats, in a traditional working-class area. The second was more difficult. It was decided that one within five miles of the first was theoretically defensible as well as a practical choice, particularly if the criterion of dominant usage by one socioeconomic group is combined with geographical location.

A constant aim in this study is to exercise a reflexivity, which means that people can make and unmake their social worlds. Not that the world does not have social patterns of meaning, or that those patterns of meanings are unrelated to relationships and values, lifestyles and social experiences which form social reality, but that a reflexive approach is required in the appraisal process.

The posh pub called the Sutcliffe Arms was middle class and adjudged by speech, dress, the cars the customers drove, and the participants. The physical space was large and expensively carpeted. One antique brass-faced clock told the correct time. The plushness of the decor was added to by dark oak tables and chairs, beamed ceilings, subdued wall lighting, and lots of antiques around on the high shelves on the walls. The bar was a straight one some distance from the door, and the door itself without the interior double door of the previous pub. There was a dining area taking up much of the room in the pub with a considerable number of chairs and tables. The public house was a meeting place of the local tennis club and had private rooms upstairs which were let for weddings and special occasions. There was a largish car park to accommodate some eighty cars and the publican's own yellow Mercedes was parked at the side of the pub - a car which was matched by those driven by customers.

Several difficulties presented themselves in the attempt to develop an observational study of the Sutcliffe Arms. Firstly - in spite of all-opening hours - the pub still opens at 7pm thus excluding an early get together by a regular male bar group. Also you were almost compelled because of the straight bar into the 'serving and selling' approach rather than the 'sitting and supping', a tradition which the brewers regard as dated and old fashioned. It meant one tall stool at each end of the bar (not two), and I could not lurk just watching, quietly observing specific encounters and interactions. The decision not to open until

7pm was the publicans, but it did have the important corollary of influencing the social usage patterns, who came with whom, why they came and what they did. It was unlikely that people 'on their way home from work' would just 'drop in'. It was discovered that major changes had been implemented some years ago when the pub had been 'improved'. The interior had been opened up and the bar straightened, at the same time as a local surge in the building of new private houses. The result had been designed to make the 'bar alteration' speed up the 'flow of service' - thus the seating at the new bar had been kept to a minimum. Thus, from my point of view there are two important differences to the previous pub; a time difference and the very shape of the bar which made getting under the 'social skin' of the pub chosen a different if not a more difficult procedure. There was one factor which was more advantageous - ordering one's drink at such a bar was a 'private affair'. I could safely disguise my pint of coke as the 'real thing' - an easier task than at the bar of the previous pub.

We have uncovered the three dimensions of social space in the previous pub, namely the open, negotiable and closed versions which were not closely linked to the physical structure. This was the scaffolding of the first pub, comprising a useful basis for analysis of what happened, the complex relationship between social groups and social usages of public-house participants. Thus in an enigmatic frame of mind the search was on for further clues which would flesh out the differences between pubs, publicans and participation patterns. So were the dimensions applicable to a second pub and if so how did they relate to the age, sex and class categories of users?

The definition of the bar area as the most open social space in a pub, where people sit or stand, and are available for encounters, was certainly the case in the second public house observed. However it was a very different kind of experience. People clustered in small knots along the bar, and the composition of such groups tended to include women in couples as well as men by themselves. There were confined interactions between couples, but very little evidence of around the bar exchange and interaction, either gestured or conversational. The conceptual notion of an open space was pervaded by the privateness of the bar experience. People interacted but there was little group sharing of stories, jokes and incidents which were important aspects in the working-class pub. People had a 'long way' to walk to the bar, and this tended to dilute the impact of a newcomer entering the pub. It also meant that people had more time to locate themselves in relation to the bar area. Sitting at the bar area was less of an opportunity for interaction, more a place where regulars sat as confidantes of tbe publican. Most of the regulars (some 70% of users) to the pub however rarely stayed at the bar itself, but tended to sit at the tables - which were numerous.

The experience of standing at the bar only allowed me to encompass small, and somewhat isolated segments of the encounters and experiences of participants. The previously cited comment by Merton that 'one cannot interact with everyone everywhere at the same time' certainly was accurate, and part of the experience of 'privateness' meant that the observation process was different and more difficult than expected. The bar was an open area and a bar group was discernible towards late evening after 9pm but not before, and it did not take on a situation like the previous pub - small groups extended from the bar into negotiable space rather than around the bar itself. 'Do it yourself' seemed the theme or focal interest, house renovation, home extension and home maintenance were a frequent topic of conversation, along with shared methods and disasters. A second focus was that of leisure projects and experiences - gardening, holidays, ventures to cricket matches, and the voluntary activities of the tennis club. Much of the discussion located itself in terms of home and family activities.

The bar group, in so far as one existed, was certainly middle class - a company secretary, a marketing director, the owner of a small garage, a chief inspector of police, a property developer, two bank managers and others. The bar could be described as an open area, there was some interaction and casual comment, aided particularly by the 'efficient sociability' of the publican who was a fund of jokes and comment. Interestingly, the publican himself evidenced a role-style which individualised his relationship with people at the bar - he did not on any occasion during the period sit at customer-side of the bar. Neither did he eat at the bar. He strictly separated his work from his non-work activities. Some attention is paid later to his role-style, but the lack of a strong bar-group seemed to be a combination of elements: the opening time of the pub; the role-style of the tenant publican; and the extent to which the bar and bar group interaction was not a focal interest of participants. It was a public social bar area of open interaction but used in a way which suggested segmented, if not private, interaction. So I ask myself which of these factors was the most influential? Having been to the pub under a previous publican when the local vicar became drunk, and the pub had been hosting an 'after the show' party, the contrast was remarkable. We shall have to wait and see, but it was about this time that I decided that I would have to interview the pub participants, observation would not be enough to explicate the situation.

The second area of social space in the working-class public house had been negotiable social space. In this first pub there was a considerable fluidity of interaction and groups between the bar and closed areas of seating and tables. However in this middle-class pub the 'negotiable social space' was much larger and very differentially negotiable. In the public house, although the space was large and commodious, it was less permeable, less casual and less fluid. Such groups were much less socially mobile, much more friendship focused. People who came into the pub - males, females, and mixed couples - tended to come together, stay together and be together. They came to the pub to enhance their own lifestyle in knots of friends, never moving very much or very far, none of the participants viewed their friends as mates or left their 'women' sitting together while they wandered around the pub.

The 'closed social space' , people getting their drinks, nodding to people they knew, and sitting at the tables, was a familiar pattern. It was very similar to the previous pub except it was extensive and gave very little impression of the implosion of social distance. The long functional bar, the location of the toilets, the absence of people sitting at the bar, the turning over of the pub to a restaurant, the turning over of the small pool area itself into yet further room for the restaurant, did not create the same kind of social experience - almost as though the segmented bar experience extended to the fest of the pub in terms of the privateness of interaction.

In comparison with the first pub the second, in terms of cross-cutting of social and physical space, shows much less of a distinction. People did not carry their pints or partners very far - even though the pub was much bigger than the previous one. The revealing contrast in the social structure of the middle-class pub is in what happened to the games area - it was used by the small proportion of working-class pub participants. It was in this area that interactional fluidity was present. It was clearly negotiable social space and functioned for the young middle-class drop outs or occasional invasions of leather-jacketed youths, who tended to arrive early on a Friday and Saturday and leave before 9pm. The tendency to create violence and tension, and amount of income to the pub, and the general uncertainty for the publican, led to its closure and replacement by another eating room.

The distinction between 'open, negotiable and closed' social space, can be added to by two further elements which impinged upon the use of the physical space of the public house. Firstly the distribution of social space appeared very much a consequence of relationships brought 'into the pub', rather then created within it. Secondly, the pub was a local in the sense that most of the regulars lived beyond walking distance and they had driven 'out' for the evening. Some knew each other well and were on first-name terms, but they were exceptional. Others were regulars who tended to fit their visits to suit their business and family schedules. These factors tended to reduce the portable nature of social space and social usage and thus the open, negotiable and closed social space was fairly static - the only exception being when the members of the tennis club held their drinking sessions, plus the occasional business meeting and disco.

Social Relationships and Sexual Stereotypes

Who met whom, why and what they did, requires intimate knowledge of participants. It requires some direct involvement in the on-going interaction pattern of relationships. The problem was one for myself - I could go into the pub and casually have a drink or a meal but that did not in itself provide an observational lurking position, and the premise for legitimised probing. The regulars were almost casuals and appeared to use the public house less as an active social base than as an extension of their existing social relations and time frameworks.

The pattern seemed all too well to fit Allan's analysis of middle-class sociability and friendship styles. Before his contention that differences in 'rules of relevance' separate the social classes, some mention should be made of the women who used the public house and how they used it. As has been declared 'there are still pubs in this country where women are not allowed to enter. These pubs - which I've come across in the North of England - have set aside special ladies lounges, as they call them with commendable delicacy, where women can be kept out of the sight of men. Arguing fiercely in my best fighting feminist manner with landlords, I have denounced this reactionary segregation. They prefer it this way, I am told. Who, I ask, are they? The men, I am assured, and the ladies. Next question; Why? Because it is patiently explained, they prefer to keep themselves to themselves. Further probing why results in shrugs and mutters of that's the way it is ... presumably this segregation nonsense is a legacy from the days when pubs were handy places for women on the make, when any woman settling herself down in a corner nursing a glass was automatically assumed to be a loose living lady on the search for clients. 'Thank goodness a woman nowadays can, at the end of a morning's battle in the supermarkets, lug her shopping into a pub, and order a reviving beverage without courting hard suspicious looks from the landlord and speculative ones from the customers' . (l) The extent to which a pub like the Sutcliffe Arms has an atmosphere which attracts women is impressive, two in five of the regulars were in this category. Is it that the good food, clean toilets, chairs rather than standing, are the secret? Given that 'women are no longer prepared to sit at home and knit and watch telly whilst their men go off alone to the pub ... many a man has had to abandon his lovable, sordid regular for something shinier and glossier and groovier, just to keep her quiet. It's a matter of self defence and simple common sense, for any sensible man realises that his only hope for domestic peace and tranquillity is his ability to keep the woman in his life happy'. (2) The women at the particular pub appeared quite at home, had no all-male bar group to negotiate, and were viewed with equality by the publican. The women would sit at the tables or less usually stand in the negotiable space. The segmented publican role style however had a very different approach for women as compared to men. He swapped jokes and information with the men, but as far as women were concerned he offered a strict sense of professional equality. In the jokes he told, including some to me when seated in the confidantes chair, were among the crudest ever heard in a public house. He had a view about women which reinforced the openness of male sufferance shown in the working-class pub - women were useful because they kept down the level of drinking, boosted the sales of meals, preferred a clean and wholesome environment, and if they kept the sex of men under control, that was a significant bonus. There was little doubt in my mind that women were useful, as far as he was concerned, but in a strict business sense. In a personal sense his views about women are almost unrepeatable - but it may depend upon the woman.

The sexual dimension in the context of the pub was not to be found in the overt bar interaction between participants, certainly usage of the bar, ordering drinks, and playing pool, was a male dominated activity. Women did stand, and sit, and were generally unassailed. Perhaps the men accepted that women were just there to have a drink, perhaps they had 'something better to do'. In fact in the middle-class pub there was no detectable sexual proposition made between the middle-class participants - except at the tennis club evening, which was by the standard of drinking at the working-class pub, a sober affair. Perhaps they were more sophisticated or less drink intoxicated, preferring an experience of segmented and individual interaction which they brought with them from home or work, and to which the public house was a follow-on process, importantly not a different process. 'Sin, song and sensuality' was a long way from a relaxed quiet evening, a 'home from home' occasion, an incidental social experience, important but not 'for itself', in terms of the opportunities it offered for activity-oriented participation in an immediate and sensual subculture. Perhaps the women going to the pub tended to view it as a process whereby they become more like the men, perhaps they viewed it as an opportunity to be equal but different, perhaps they saw it as a situation of inequality which would never be put right without changing the economic class system. I was beginning to find that I had started by a belief in a class system as a basis for stratification, but events were carrying me towards a gender basis which was more profound than class.

The Publican's Role

Sydney was in his mid-forties, had been at the pub for some nine years, and a publican for fifteen. His wife had left him - it began to be an occupational trait - and he had living at the pub a friend and his two children aged seventeen and twenty. Prior to the publican's role, he had been a car salesman and managed a garage, and still had a range of contacts in the car business. He very much viewed the pub as a business, and viewed his customers as coming to the pub for 'peace and privacy in a pleasant environment'. We adopt the same scheme as with the first pub, an interest in the publican/customer relationship, and the publican! family dimension, as observed and centred around the role of the publican himself.

Gentle Publican and Gentle Customers

The way he related to 'the regulars' of his pub was very much as a professional to other professionals. He rarely anticipated the drinks of his regulars - he only came into contact with them when they reached the bar. What was interesting about the publican was that he did not put his regulars into any format - what they were drinking depended upon where they had come from, the time in the evening it was, who else was with them - a sight of the door from the bar, and double door entry as at the previous pub, would have given the opportunity for him to make a judgement. He did not do so, partly because he did not know who was' coming in' , partly because he made no assumptions about their status or need - plus which he was aware of' drinking and driving' . He was prepared to respond to the customer's initiation, rarely to be the initiator. His specialised knowledge of cars was one information linkage of some importance and formed a brief across the bar interaction encounter. He would engage in some 'across the bar' chat but would break it off to deal with a customer who 'appeared suddenly' at the bar. There seemed to be no exclusion or inclusion strategies but the way he regarded men and women as customers, and the ways he joked to the men about the women that they were with in terms of sexual stereotypes - women were objects to be used or misused but never confronted with such a male definition of them - was unmistakable. There were thus deployed by the publican customer information and joking strategies, with special customers as individuals not as members of a group.

The interesting fact of the publican's role was how little he had to demonstrate control over what was normative deregulation in a situation where 'anything happened' during the period of observation. Perhaps it was because the publican drank little - after 9pm and much weakened whisky. Perhaps it was because most of the participants were not looking for 'excitement' or casual encounters. By 11pm on a Friday or Saturday, with a brisk closing of the bar, people had usually 'cooled themselves out' of the situation - either by having a meal, going on to a club, or going home. It was a 'respectable' pub and rather unexciting when compared to the rumbustious situation previously experienced.

Fitting the Pub in with the Family

In comparison with the respectable working-class pub, there were several advantages which the Sutcliffe Arms had. Firstly the publican and his family lived beside the pub, not over it. Unlike the previous pub therefore there was no 'spillover' from the work side to the home side of what was going on, unlike the 'respectable' working class pub. Access to the family living area was via the dining area through the kitchen, and thus there was a physical division between the pub area and the home area of the public house. Thus the family could go 'in and out' of the pub but the customers could only enter and exit through the pub door. The Sutcliffe Arms had its own separate 'front door' a reinforcing element keeping the 'work side' and the 'family side' of the pub separate. The general effect was that the family members and their friends, and the publican when 'off duty' could come and go without interacting with the pub participants. Secondly, the publican did not have a young family likely to precipitate a constant domestic crises. He had had 'enough of kids' he said, and did not think his customers came to his pub to be presented with a family situation. The third element of some importance was that although he had a partner - of sorts - he maintained a clear separation of his relationship with her when in the public house. People knew she was not his 'wife' but could only guess at their relationship. Thus few personal differences between the couple were ever in the open, although her occasional absence at busy times could be attributable to such conflict.

The family was importantly involved in running the Sucliffe Arms. Sheila, the wife, was mainly responsible for the meals side of the pub, both at lunchtime and in the evenings. On occasions she was helped by the daughter, whilst the older son helped out at the bar. On Fridays and at weekends the family ran the pub. The social division of family labour on a weekly basis was fairly clear. The publican was never there all day on a Tuesday or Wednesday, midweek being fairly quiet, and his regulars did not expect to see him before Wednesday evening, making the most of a midweek break in the running of the pub. Usually it was Alf who stood in for him, a semi-retired barman of long standing and a personal friend, who took over and 'ran' the pub. All of the family were in attendance when the pub opened on Friday and Saturday, and stayed for much of the time depending how busy the pub was. The family bar staff always dressed 'smartly' - not as if they lived next door at all, and it was part of Sydney's insistence on maintaining standards - something of which he was proud. Sydney explained that his sort of customers would not come into a shoddy pub, and since he ran it he expected the same standards from family as well as non-family staff. He himself, even when dressed casually, looked 'smart'. The pub itself was always smart and clean and in an attempt to gain some access to the family residence, to obtain some sense of the impingement of the work side of running the pub and the home (out of hours) the writer of this book went to buy a bottle of whisky. Access was gained to the front room of the residence of 'the house'. It was neat without the evidence of domestic chaos and 'things everywhere'.

The findings reported tend to confirm that the Sutcliffe Arms was a middle-class public house. By and large it confirms Allan's claim in respect of participation, activity and usage patterns. The crucial variables appeared to be the combination of two dimensions, the importance of private and personal interaction and the non-centrality of the public house as a focus of public sociability. For the middle class thus the social context did appear to be a 'public situation of private interaction', as contrasted with a working-class use of the pub as a 'private situation of public interaction' . At least that appeared to lay to rest a class basis for the pub. There appeared however a fundamental issue which was becoming more significant and profound than that of class. It was that of gender differences, men and women in a public leisure context which is freely available to all. Some questions were raised earlier in this chapter about why women were so denigrated and 'put down' by the men involved. There are various answers, depending upon where one is standing and what one sees. I am more convinced than when I started the search for some answers to the part the pub plays in our society, that part of the enigma involves women and an appraisal of what they expect. Perhaps we have a double helix in which the public house is only one strand, in the debate between work and masculinity in the class analysis. The second strand is the women and men issue. Why is it that women appear so belittled when it comes to usages of various kinds of pubs? Is the pub an alternative to home and family in some circumstances? We shall see what the interviews reveal and then draw some conclusions. We now turn to the 'rough' underclass public house - a third type which was uncovered during the attempt to discover a classification of pubs.

Chapter 7 References

1. McGill Angus (Ed)., Pub: A Celebration, Longmans Green and Co., London, Proops Marjorie, 'What will you have, Mrs Pankhurst?', 1969 pl26

2. Ibid pl27

Chapter 8

The 'Rough' Underclass Public House

The 'rough pub' is one which emerged in the research process. I was not sure that I wanted to go further - I had enough material, and one more type of public house would not make that much difference.

Enough material for what? I had some clues and had 'peeled back' some of the differences between the respectable working-class and the posh middle class pubs. What good would I do by seeking a pub which was at the end of the continuum? Perhaps I just wanted to know - there was no doubt about the true nature of the enigma. Perhaps I had become obsessed by a lurking suspicion that I had yet to capture the context of perpendicular drinking, criminality, tough masculine values and a beer sodden culture - so much part of the image of the pub in the social conditions of Victorian England. Perhaps I was just like Alice seeking the origin of the smile on the face of the Cheshire cat. And it was still strange to realise that having begun to explain one mystery, the pub, I had suddenly stumbled upon another; the consequences of being a woman in a public-house world. Women are treated differently to men, are perceived differently, are regarded as separate and threatening - and the pub is the context in which this is worked out. The mystery of how far at institutional and interactionable levels women can become the property of pubs, the hold that men have over them rather than the freedom that women deserve, required further analysis. The rough pub may pose the problem at an acute level - we shall see what transpires.

A Rough Underclass Pub

The flaunting image of the public house compensating for all of the baneful things about urban life, the poverty, insecurity, squalid housing, tyrannous mechanised laboUT, inadequate education, poor health, bound-up with criminality, promiscuity and sexual exploitation, it was no wonder that such a rough pub was viewed with some degree of apprehension. The pub regulars from the working-class pub, told an interesting story - about the reputation of one local pub, such that 'no respectable person would go into that pub', a place frequented by 'mad buggers and head bangers'. The picture of Roger and Mary sipping their respective pint and larger in the oak-beamed Rose and Crown, sharing in the controlled conviviality of the situation, contrasted sharply with the 'sawdust on the floor' conjured up by a rough pub. Where was the 'civilising morality' in an ethos of rational recreation, of creating 'wholesome behaviour in wholesome environments'? A casual visit to the Fox and Hounds, to see if it revealed any further clues about the role of the public house in contemporary society, about types of users, the gender of the culture, the role of the publican or the sociability dynamics of the pub, evoked its inclusion. It would have been unjustifiable and unimaginative not to attempt an appraisal of such a pub. On the first casual visit to the pub it was discovered that the publican had a 'record as long as yer arm', and circulating at the bar, from the bin man, was a range of well-thumbed pornographic literature, which revealed the maleness of the sexual stereotyping of women and the dominantly masculine culture of the public house concerned.

The location of the public house was to be found in a typical run-down area. The affluence of once busy small manufacturing concerns and 'clean front doorsteps' of quite smart terraced houses had given way to planning blight areas of bulldozed housing and others awaiting slum clearance. It was a depressing grey area reminiscent of the kind of description of 'Luke Street' on Merseyside, and the rough pub, Casey's, which was studied by Gill in his explanation of a delinquent subculture. 'Luke Street accommodation is poor and crowded. Casey's offers a refuge from the stresses of living in such conditions. When the men go into Casey's they take it easy and family responsibilities will not intrude on their enjoyment. They can drink, play darts, and talk. Talk about what's happened at work and in the street. Talk about what the boss said to someone. He's a cunt him. Talk about what the corporation haven't done. Wankers driving big Rovers and not deserving a penny. Talk about the police. Bastards, never met a decent one. But most of all talking about sport .. if you live in Luke Street you don't need an excuse to go into Casey's. Going in for a drink is a good enough explanation .. .in its time it would have been a respectable pub sharing in a modest way in the prosperity of the town ... as a result of its age, the decline of the town and recent housing and industrial development in its immediate surroundings, the pub has changed into a depressing comer pub in a physically depressing state'. (l)

The Fox and Hounds had much of the locational feel of Casey's and shared some of the physical characteristics of the first pub studied - small, tenanted and with the home above the pub. It was divided into three areas, a bar-lounge area, a second social area and a pool room. It was a garishly tatty pub, with low copper-topped tables, creamy going brown paint work and although once carpeted, the carpet was well worn and in places holes had been covered up. The wallpaper was torn from the wall in places and there were two clocks, one permanently stopped at 12 o'clock and one a quarter of an hour fast. The pub boasted two space invader machines, a juke box, a gaming machine and a television - it felt crowded even when there were few people present. Before describing paterns of users and usage, during the period of observation, it is important to highlight several aspects of the process. Going into the pub, ordering a drink and standing at the bar, was viewed as a mildly provocative act by the 'regulars' . Joining the pub as part of the supposedly' open group' at the bar he was informed that he 'could not stand there' because it was Tommy's spot 'he'll shift ya when he's in'. Tommy was 'in' fairly soon and since he was about twice the size of myself I decided that situational tact was the better part of sociological valour - I shifted. Just how regular the situation was to the men concerned revealed also how closed the bar was to outsiders. It took the situation with analysis of the working-class bar one step further - even the bar was 'closed'. The second fact was indicated by whose right it was to sit on the bar stool, there being only one at the end of the bar - it was reserved for the 'king' as regulars called him, the man who could 'take out' any other in the pub. The third interesting aspect of entry to the pub - as subsequently become clearer - was my reaction to the pornographic literature. My offer to have it 'reprinted' meant that I was regarded as a 'fucking good un' and accepted, albeit my rough clothes did not match my less-rough voice. It might help that I had thought about being accepted as an 'unemployed maths teacher' and that seemed to satisfy the regulars. Two other aspects revealed themselves in the first few weeks of going to the pub - one about the role style of the publican, a second relating to the family tensions in running the pub.

The publican - Bill - was behind the bar less often than in front of it, the regulars complaining that he was 'never there'. Dennis the bin man poured my first pint - not coke. Bill was usually found playing pool at lunchtimes and early evenings, or running a gambling card group late at night, with the young male regulars - with one or two women attached to the group. The card group was a situation where everything was 'fucking' with the publican being central to the group. In terms of marital tension, Bill quite freely shared with the bar group his marriage conflicts. His wife was not talking to him during the first week of my observation. It became increasingly obvious throughout the period she was subject to considerable conflict in terms of the running of the pub and looking after the house 'upstairs', with one eight year old child. (2)

Social Dimensions of the Pub

The three dimensions of the first working-class pub were not totally applicable. Given the discovery of the bar area, the dinning area and the games area, as the three distinct spaces in the first pub, things in the third pub were not so distinct.

There was no distinct dining area, the pub served snacks and these could be eaten anywhere in the pub. The physical space of the pub was distinctly not separate, partly because of the gaming machine sited at the physical intersection of the three rooms. People playing the machines could see and be seen, and heard, where ever one was in the pub. Also because the pub had been 'opened up' the adjoining room furthest from the bar, could be clearly seen. The physical space was small and two external doors had been bricked up, which used to, according to the regulars, be the entrances to the taproom and the snug. The existing front door access meant that the customer could be seen clearly from the bar, and it was the only access. The experience of the physical space being permanently not separate was added to by a large beer barrel which served as a standing-at-surface, and was placed centrally in the negotiable area of the pub. The most physically separate area of the pub was the games room, which was not visible from the bar and which had a door that was occasionally closed. My strategy with this third pub was threefold; firstly to become a member of the bar group which formed about 4.30pm to 7pm; secondly to return to the pub about 8.30pm through to closing time on weekdays and weekends; and thirdly to visit at lunchtimes from 12.30pm to 3pm staying earlier or somewhat later with a particular focus on midweek and weekends. The period of observation was three months for the rough pub, as opposed to six months for the posh pub and nine months for the respectable pub. It was thought that this fmal public house might show in what sense this enigmatic institution was similar to how the public house used to be - and to a large extent it did.

The first question we asked of both previous pubs was what relationship existed between physical space and the actual social usage of the space - open, negotiable and closed social space were the categories uncovered. In the rough pub about 98% of users were regulars - they came more than once a week. All of those who came were male manual workers, unemployed or women who visited the pub 'on the look out', including Susan who several of the regulars regarded as the 'biggest slag in the place'. When they came in, and what they did, seemed very little related to the physical structure of the pub in terms of designated usage. In fact it seemed like the largish room in the early nineteenth century, with a place to get your drink, was a place to remind yourself, or forget the pressures of life, and talk - and like most regulars in such pubs the place for women was bed and breakfast, and not going into the pub except to find a man. There were only two groups which were obvious; the young male 'tough' regulars up to 25 and the older group, aged 35 plusalso all male - both groups by themselves. The younger males tended to play the machines and pool, and were the regulars in the card gambling sessions. The older males tended to form a distinct bar group, always standing at the bar which was designed for them - it was in the form of a quarter circle so that in theory anyone who wanted could join in the talk at any time. The older men were generally large drinkers - some as much as fifteen pints, while I modestly stuck to my two and a half pints. About 60% of regulars walked to the pub, the others arriving by van, bus and waggon - the 'king' came by waggon, and he was twice the size of Steve (the kings's mate), and Steve was twice my own physical size. They were both builders' labourers and there appeared a fairly strict male ranking order around the bar; Sid sat at the end of the bar presiding, Steve stood half way along the bar whilst I and an unemployed engineer - a lathe turner - stood at the end of the bar, I myself being of unknown and unproven qualities. The two groups, the male middle-aged bar group and the tough male youngsters were the pub regulars, along with an itinerant group of women, often coming in by themselves, standing at the bar dressed to kill, buying one drink, very conspicuously doing nothing but standing at the bar. Susan was a regular coming on Tuesday, Friday and Saturday at about 7pm and there were some other 'regular' women who arrived after 9pm, sometimes leaving by themselves, sometimes not. Very occasionally a middle-class couple, to judge by dress and speech, wandered into the pub and usually survived one drink, even on one occasion deciding not to have a drink, but standing, looking and rapidly leaving. It was a contrast to the other working-class pub and worlds away from the Sutcliffe Arms and middle-class suburbia.

To assert that there was little relationship between the social and physical space in the pub, was puzzling. Were the categories evolved in relation to the first public house not relevant to the Fox and Hounds, the rough pub? Were the observer strategies adopted different, and thus the vantage point from which social usage patterns viewed different? It was suddenly realised that in a social situation where virtually all participants were regulars, were known to each other, almost exclusively male and rough working class, with only a small proportion of women as appendages, sitting watching 'their men' play cards, waiting to be picked up or involved in sexual interaction in a comer - such as the couple who sat astride each other for a long period one night - was a situation dominated by one element of social space. It was all predominantly a 'private' situation of homogenous group interaction of private focal interests. It was as though the maleness and focal interests of the bar group extended to the entire pub. The sociability dynamics were along the same sociability dimension. It almost reminded me of the pre-industrial man, living in his own world, developing his own theories, giving rewards to his own kind, creating his own social distance and acceptance. Men as men, drinking a great deal, swearing freely, meeting regulars whom they regarded as drinking mates. They saw themselves, in themselves, as their own world. The paradox of both an 'open' and yet 'closed' group was not because they wanted privacy, or because there were age and class groupings, but because it was 'one' class public house, precarious and temporary but it survived upon immediacy and sensuality. The fact that it was wholly a male group made me wonder about the place of women, if the situation was reversed, would it be the same? It showed that it had become a one class public house, part of the undermass in the terrain of working-class culture. This realisation suggests that the closed social space which was typical of the posh middle-class pub, related to the individualised and segmented lifestyles was, instead of being devolved downwards, related upwards to the total membership of the pub, the pub physical situation and the whole pub area constituted such a closed collective space usage for the regulars. Thus it constituted vitality within the pub freedom, but outside the pub existed a strong sense of fatalism for the men struggling to survive. The pub groupings which had visibly made sense in the respectable pub and had reduced and stabilised in the posh pub, just did not exist in the rough pub. What men did in the rough pub was not differentiated enough to be portable. I suggest that three elements made this possible: firstly no separate areas where what the regulars did was supposed to happen; secondly you could drink, eat a snack, 'make love', play the machines, or watch telly, wherever and when ever you wished; thirdly the role style of the publican was integrated in terms of playing pool, running the card sessions, and 'returning' to the bar occasionally. All of these elements fostered the permanent social experience of 'private openness' and lead to the potential deregulation of accepted social norms - especially if, as in a pub, the very act of drinking may change how the situation is perceived. In short the extent to which a pub identifies its space, the tighter the publican professionally controls what is available, the more that its regulars come into apparently free yet an organised situation, the closer one comes to a middle-class conception of the public house. Patterns of activity, participation and interaction thus become crystallised in terms of any particular public house. However the public house still poses some distinct problems.

Social Relationships and Sexual Stereotypes

The attempt to disentangle the social relationships - who met whom, why and what they did, and links of the pub participants to non-public house relation networks - in the two pubs prior to the rough pub, only gradually unfolded.

In the rough pub there was a clear masculine hierarchy. It was age differentiated in that whilst physical strength and drinking capacity were the two distinct elements, they operated differently accordingly to the two age groups of males dominating the pub itself. For the young men, often the skinheads or denim or leather jacketed, masculine competition focused around the games, pool, cards and space invader machines, rather than drinking itself. Many were unemployed and looked as though they were under the age of drinking so did not locate themselves at the bar. Thus 'the local lads are really neophytes in a world of job insecurity, bad housing and not enough money ... they're learning that life isn't going to offer you much, but what it does offer you'll take. No one will stand in the way of what pleasure there is. Casey's is where you learn that. Unemployment, the man at the job shop said they'd be lucky if they got anything at the moment. Better make the most of it. Don't want to move .. .its all they know. Somebody said join the army. Come talk at school. Travel, sport. Fuck that. They're wearing the same denims they wear all the time. No money for the best clothes. Just full-time denims. Close cropped hair, denim jackets, denim jeans and big boots'. (2) It was such a group at the Fox and Hounds which played the punk-rock and heavy metal music on the juke box, which on occasions took over the pool area as its distinct territory for affirming their all male subcultural identity. Most of the 'lads' were locals, had been academic rejects at school, at the pub they were 'doing nothing', rarely talking - except to 'fuck' everything, and play for pints. The pub seemed to offer some relief to the boredom of living, to being involved in the tough maleness of the bar group world of male power, status and drinking, with the experience that women played no part in the maleness of such a world. The transition from the young group of regulars to the bar group was fairly ritualised via the card game - usually five card stud or poker. The invitation to join the group was at the discretion of the publican himself, and becoming a member of the group signified a step in the hierarchy of masculine values and membership acceptance.

The second major group of pub users were the older males, almost without exception by themselves. The extent of 'known-ness' of this group to each other was remarkable. Some were employed in the same firm or in the same kind of work - they were predominantly labourers from around Newcastle. There were a number - three or four - who were laid off from the building trade, as well as a number of other marginal occupations, including Fred the rent man, John who was a tailor's fitter, a railway porter, Dennis the bin man and Stan who was on the sick - and looked it. Relationships appeared to be very much occupationally based, and they seemed to use the pub as a 'home from work' to talk about work problems - compensation, insurance, redundancy, 'making money on the side', as well as gambling, horse racing, and cars. There was very little discussion about women, perhaps because they were not around or perhaps the men had resolved how to deal with them. Although there was bar pornography it was not subject to witty comment or jokes in terms of sexual stereotyping. There was no telephone in the pub area, so no wives or lovers phoned. The nearest was children coming to the pub door, asking for' Dad' to tell him that 'tea was ready' . There was little ambiguity about how women were defined - 'women, fucking cows' and little talk at the bar about wives, marriages or sexual adventures. It was almost as though the group at the bar 'did things' rather than talked about them. There was a very clear self image of 'men as men' and work as labour, and much focus on survival in a situation of poverty, hardship and economic-social inequality. The bonds born of the uncertainty of work seem much akin to Jackson's view of the 'deep and terrible rhythm of poverty as the grounds of working- class life'.

The realisation of the consequences of poverty perhaps led to Stan - on the sick - being readily accepted in the hierarchy of bar life. He would not be sent to the 'infirmary' the regulars assured him, and they freely lent him money without any expectation of being repaid. And those relationships extended to the family and the 'women folk' who came in on Friday and Saturday night, mainly after 8pm. The older women came in twosomes, joining their husbands, not by sitting or standing with them but in the sense of being there together. The language changed for the night and the situation was a conjoining of the separate worlds, with older children being allowed in as part of the family sharing process, sitting around with their 'Mums'. The men were dressed 'casually-smart' for the occasion. The 'king' was smart and shaved, Dennis the bin man with his blue woolly hat was nowhere to be seen, even Stan looked different, and the occasion had all the hallmarks of celebration and festivity.

Not all the women on a Saturday were older and married. Acolytes of the young male neophytes were to be found, usually in twosomes, but without their regular boyfriends, and forming a parallel grouping. The situation reminded me of the Worktown Study except that the pub was transformed into a lounge, even to the extent of some of the older women standing at the bar and taking on jokes about their hairstyles and lack of drinking capacity. Tina, who was Bill's wife, adopted a protectionist attitude towards women who came into the pub. It was she who put the regular males in their place both in terms of language and behaviour. It was Tina who ran the bar for most of the week and although Bill was around the bar on Friday and Saturday, it was when Bill's sister came in, thus Bill was still infrequently behind the bar. One of the most interesting factors in the Saturday night festivity was a visit to the pub, of 'not very nice girls' , as Tina described the prostitutes who came into the pub on a client-tripping routine. I decided that trying to chat up the women, to get picked up by one of the 'not very nice girls', might be one step beyond the pub remit. It was possible to watch them - how did they manage the situation in an all male world? There was a three step strategy: firstly a clear social visibility approach - they were 'dressed up to the nines', a very distinct contrast when compared to the other women who came into the pub. They stood alone at the bar, usually not for too long; secondly, a public non-involvement approach, the women tended not to initiate any conversation, bought their own drinks and waited to be approached; thirdly, they operated a selective client approach, they did not allow themselves to be picked-up by just 'anyone'. Given the number of single male clients to the pub, it became clear that according to the women concerned they had established clients at the pub whom they preferred and waited for in the pub. Usually the 'pick-up' involved the minimum of conversation, such as 'shall we go somewhere else'? And the couple walked out through the pub doors to another pub, but who knows, perhaps not.

There is some explanation as to 'why' the situation exists, who met whom and what they did, and it should yield some clues. It suggests that a fairly narrow range of values and interests were operative. The pub was a refuge from the uncertainty of life experiences, the harshness of work as labour, as paid employment, as part of the male toughness of 'making a living'. Don't women share such experiences I wondered? Certainly the toughness of work was added to for women by the insensitivity of family and the stress of human relationships. The men had found or created an acceptable way out. The gathering of ragged men, mostly wearing their working clothes, an odd collection of woolly jumpers, worn jeans, ubiquitous anoraks, with sported woolly hats - reputedly made from worn out jumpers - portrayed a visual roughness. The experience of the pub appeared to result in the immediacy of sharing together in the maleness of a man's world, and a blurring of the edges of social reality in the levity and forgetfulness induced by drink. And it is drink alcohol in all its forms to which we shall return to in our conclusion. It was a world in which women could share - on male terms - the wives on Friday and Saturday evenings and the 'not very nice girls' as part of the availability of sex for money. The participants were hard drinkers but rarely was it a situation in which drunkenness and violence occurred. Part of 'being a man' was to be able to 'hold your drink', and to 'take women if you wanted to', and to exploit in the outside world the economic arrangements which are themselves repressive and exploitative, not to use the pub to assert male virility which required little demonstration - the 'king' was usually on his bar room stool. The most drunken behaviour was in the 'fucking' language which was certainly uninhibited. What held the regulars together was the contrast between the pub as a world of certainty, mates, fuddled joy, accepted male values, and uncertainty of the outside world beyond the pub. The Fox and Hounds was an oasis of certainty for the regulars, an ordered world of understood communality, as compared to a hostile and uncertain world. 'Uncertainty leads to a number of things. First it leads to a philosophy of live now, to enjoy yourself while you can. The realities of life ... are not conducive to a philosophy of deferred gratification. There is a sense offatalism and making the best of life. Secondly it leads to a situation in which you don't look down your nose at the bloke you are with - you might be next. Thirdly it leads to helping out - seeing somebody right for a couple of weeks. Finally the irregular employment leads to "making a few bob" .. doing small one-off jobs for other people or the expression could have more directly illegal connotations'. (3) I myself have strong views that the rough pub explained most of the mystery surrounding the pub. That view may be conditioned on the part women have, will have and could play in the pub, and crucially upon the participant part of the publican.

Customer and Family Relationships of the Publican

The situation in the rough pub was little related to the situation which was discovered by Campbell in the account of pubs : 'Good evening, I said. May I have a large whisky and some ginger wine? Plain water I added, after a moment. It had no effect upon her of any kind. She continued to sit on the stool. The variegated red face went on beaming at me. The old man in the public bar again decided to be helpful. "Screws gotter", he said, then added in a kindly way, "pore ole Nell". Suddenly he shouted, "Fraid"! Followed a moment later by, "Shop"! He relapsed once more. He seemed to have made little impression on the glass of brown ale. This time fully five minutes appeared to go by before the curtain was agitated again. When it did move it moved almost imperceptibly and then, almost as if he'd walked through it, a little old man with a pale bald head was standing in front of it. He wore two dark waistcoats over a tattered grey cardigan. On his face was a look of surprised apprehension as though he'd been summoned without warning from bed to take charge of a fatal accident. "Good evening", I said. "I'm sorry to disturb you but could I have a large whisky with some ginger - and plain water?" He looked at me in astonishment for quite a while. His expression now suggested that something like an ostrich had walked into his pub and had started asking, it might be the English language, for a drink. "Just a whisky would do", I said, trying to break it up a bit, "if you haven't got the ginger wine". The ostrich, or whatever it was, had spoken again, further deepening the mystery. He turned his astonished gaze upon poor old Nell but she had no suggestions to offer. He decided upon action. He left me standing in the saloon bar, and shuffled slowly into the public bar. "Wanta nuvver, Charlie?" He asked the old man. "Not yet, Fraid", the old man said. He came to the conclusion that a more elaborate explanation was necessary. "Aven't fmished one I got," he said, pointing to it. Fraid hung around a bit longer, waiting perhaps for Charlie to finish his drink, but Charlie showed no sign of wishing even to pick it up. Fraid, baffled and defeated, rearranged some dirty glasses on the counter and then appeared to steel himself for the ordeal'. (4) At least at the rough pub I was a participant customer and was used to serving myself a drink - if only because he was 'never there', to quote Dennis the bin man. There seemed to be a high degree of ambivalence by Bill to explain his behaviour. However I could derive quite a lot from the observation strategy. Being an unemployed maths teacher I was invited into the card group and also played pool on occasions.

The publican had had the pub for four and a half years but left much of the running of the pub to his wife. Lunchtimes he was rarely to be seen and he had a very variable schedule for the teatime trade, and even for Friday and Saturday evenings. There seemed a very unequal division of the work side of the public house between Bill and Tina. It was she who was more likely to be collecting glasses, making snacks, and hosting the regulars. The publican himself tended to 'drift around' the pub and seemed to pursue an almost totally informal relationship with the regulars, being found in the card group, playing pool, playing the more expensive of the two space-invader machines. When I asked quite casually why he didn't stay behind the bar, the publican said that he 'didn't fucking need to' , and where he was at any time 'didn't fucking matter'. He was correct in that he was within five or six paces of the bar wherever he was. Bill 'was' the publican and rather than separating himself from the regulars, integrated himself with them in a relational sense, but because of the relationship he had with his wife, he reckoned there was more income to be made outside the pub - on his various deals outside in the second-hand car market. Doing deals outside the pub, sitting in other pubs, and playing pool and cards, encouraging the big drinkers, was a summary of his contribution. Tina who effectively ran the pub usually gave Bill a cool reception and held the view that 'the worst mistake we ever made was taking a pub', and this was reinforced by Bill's own unpredictability. It was instructive when they were both at the bar at the same time. Bill gave the 'orders' and Tina was 'required to comply' - and regulars just nodded into their glasses signalling either their approval of the male structure of power, or not wanting to be involved. Tina found it difficult to cope with the takeover of family life by public-house life.

There was very little trouble at the pub during the amount of time I spent there. Certainly, with the amount of time I spent there, there ought to have been. The effect of high alcohol consumption was to create a rowdy scene with loud voices, colourful language, people falling about or gradually subsiding as they propped up the bar. None of the behaviour however fitted the 'head bangers' and 'mad buggers' description. However there was a rich mythology of what had happened in the past; how the 'king' had 'taken out challengers to his supremacy'. Perhaps the most celebrated and repeated tale was what happened on the anniversary. Bill and Tina had laid out a special feast for the regulars on a Saturday evening. Three of the regulars had been drinking at the pub since lunchtime and had continued with a bottle of whisky into the early evening. They had a Chinese meal for which they had 'forgotten' to pay. As a result they were chased by the Chinese cook with a meat cleaver and in the Chinese way had been 'blessed'. They found that the anniversary had made the pub very popular, so much so they could not 'get at the food' which had been laid out for the regulars. They decided to 'lift' the side of beef from the spread. Having sobered up from drinking by the next morning they 'phoned the pub and told them the 'beef was tough'. For this exploit they were barred for the whole of the following week.

In one sense it was a deregulated context. What the regulars did was not consistent with expectations. It would have been out of place at either of the other two pubs, as it was formally in the Fox and Hounds. It might have been acceptable at the bar of the working-class pub. It was accepted however within the framework of maleness and hard drinking of the rough pub concerned - the three regulars were only barred for one week. I wondered what the regulars would have to do to be stopped from coming for six months. In part, what was permitted, being that it was an unwritten book of behaviour where immediacy and masculinity were the participants' focal interests?

Chapter 8 References

1. Gill 0., Luke Street, Macmillan, 1977, p79

2. Ibidp80

3. Ibidp84

4. McGill Angus (ed)., Pub: A Celebration, Longmans, pI55 Patrick Campbell, 'They've absolutely ruined it', London, 1969

Chapter 9

Talking with the Working Class About Their Participation

I t is bold to try and interview the participants of the pubs concerned. They might do, say and be anything. They might refuse to be interviewed. I gained the confidence of the pub regulars with patience and trust.

None of the names used are the actual names. It involved taping and working through with a list of headings which actually represented differences in the past and present circumstances of public houses. It also makes an assessment of what the participants felt and thought about the pub and how they experienced the times they spent in the pub. Did drinking provide the basic reason for going to the pub? What about entertainment, what about sociability? What about the women in these pubs, how did they relate to the situation? Finally, what sort of difference did the publican make? These are difficult questions. But not impossible as we shall see.

In view of the increasing place and pace of women's freedom, did the nature of the public house become nearer, less ambiguous for women? What is increasingly important, did the ignoring of the public house by sociology appear defensible, particularly in the light of the number of pubs there are and the quantity of people who drink in them. To ignore such contexts, the different ways they shape, modify and change behaviour, and the special role they have for the specifics of work leisure relationships, and the work family relationships, are not to be ignored. Complexity is no excuse for ignoring the institution which plays such an important role in contemporary society.

There are various ways of conceptually slicing interview data. As already suggested, for the sake of clarity and because it was not a concern with 'quantifrenia', the findings reveal two sharp overwhelming questions: firstly are pub usages class stratified?; secondly are pub usages gender oriented? Therefore the manual and non-manual occupational categories, and male and female gender categories, are used.

The Male Working-Class Customers

1. Where, When and How of Pub Usage

The male manual workers - the male working-class element interviewed visited the pub at least three times a week, often more frequently. Visiting was almost exclusively during the evening and concentrated especially on Thursday, Friday and Saturday evenings, although some went to the pub every evening. They all regarded the pub as a local at which they were regulars, they each had two or three other pubs however, in which they were regulars.

Ted was aged twenty two, a motor mechanic, unmarried and a frequent participant of the rough pub. He explained: 'I visit the pub four nights a week. I've got four local pubs and my nearest is about a mile from my home, the furthest is about five miles. I'm a biker and always drive. I never go to pubs at lunchtimes and never before eight o'clock at night. On a night out I go to all four pubs starting at the one furthest from home.'

Clive was aged nineteen, a labourer, unmarried and a regular at the Nelson. He said: 'I live about a mile and a half from the pub, always drive, after I finish work I always go home for my tea, do jobs and then go out for a bit of entertainment. I go to the pub - to the pub every night, usually start at or finish up the local'.

Tommy aged thirty four was a brickie, married with three children under twelve and very much part of the Fox and Hounds tea-time bar group. He explained 'I come in most nights on the way home. Sometimes I stop off at the Mutton, but I likes it here - it's me second home. Me mates, we have a drink and a good laugh, no fucking women nor kids. I comes back later for the cards. Yeah, it's me local- what a fucking daft question. Drive, yeah, but I walks back later. '

Russell amplified the picture somewhat, aged thirty one, a postman, married with two children and a regular at the Nelson. 'On average I go to a pub four or five times a week, several times to my local, more often than not finish there for the last pint or two. Sometimes I walk, sometimes I drive. I might decide to only come to this pub you know, come about nine o'clock, and stay till closing time. Having an early start to work, you know, I can't stop to the bitter end. It might vary a little bit but it sort of depends. I might bump into someone and therefore stop a bit longer. I don't really have an evening routine. Lunchtime is a bit different, I usually call Friday lunchtime just for the odd pint or two, not a skinful, maybe because I'm going out at night, you know, the lads we generally get together, four or five of us at the end of the week. I really prefer to drink at night. '

For Brian, fifty two, a divorced mechanic, with one married daughter and a regular at the Nelson, added to the information by telling me: 'I go to the pub in the evening, sometimes walk, sometimes drive. I go to a lot of different pubs but usually visit my local three or four times a week. I don't necessarily stay for long and might go on to two or three other pubs. I usually go to a pub anytime from 4.30pm onwards.'

Several important features emerged from such comments. Firstly the men were pub regulars, very regular. Secondly, they obviously were regulars at more than one pub, often three or four. Thirdly the married men at least indicated they arrived at some sort of compromise with their 'woman' over the pub-going out with 'your mates' on a Friday or Saturday night.

2. Why They Visited the Pub and Types of Pub

Each of the regular male participants was asked why they visited the pub what were the three most important reasons for them going? Each of them was not expected to rank the order of such reasons, but having said that, it is surprising when one looks at the consistency of the reasons.

Terry, aged thirty, who was an unemployed van driver, unmarried and who was a regular at the Nelson said: 'I suppose I go out many a time thinking I might meet me mates or the right girl, the number one reason is company. Second, the beer, I like drinking. You know, I mean, I like to taste what I am drinking. Its magic just to stand there and pour it down. Number three is pool, I go to make money, to do some hustling for the pool job. ' Terry appeared to make quite a lot of money from playing pool- some eighty or ninety games a week, going to different pubs, but usually starting or finishing at the Nelson.

Clive was also clear why he went to the pub. 'To get out of the house, its boring sat there with your mother, what good is that? I go to see my pals, bit of a crack, a laugh. It's no good if you 're just sat there is it? People don't go into pubs to drink. They can't afford. They go for company more than drink. '

Russell, the postman said: 'I like the atmosphere of pubs. I go for a chat, to unwind, to relax, to have a drink you know, its nice to bump into one of my mates. If I go to the local its inevitable I do and, you know, after a day's work I just unwind in the pub. '

Ted was equally clear too as to why he went to the pub: 'I go to catch up on gossip, to meet my buddies. I don't pick up women in pubs. I go out to meet folk I normally meet and see what's happened. '

Tommy graphically said he went to his pub because 'it's a fucking good place. I can meet the lads and 'ave a good pint 'afore tea and I'm bored to bleeding death with TV an' kids'.

All the men going to the pub had high to their list meeting people they knew their mates, mostly people they met in the pub itself with whom they shared a communality of interests and values. Drinking was important but the pub provided an escape to a different kind of world, no bosses, no women, no TV and no kids, the certainty of meeting mates with whom gossip and information could be exchanged, confidences swapped, and with whom they could relax

-literally opt out of a time-constrained and routinised world, alcohol aided if not alcohol induced. The pub, from the comments of these regulars, was a place for making and reaffirming their social links. What was interesting was to learn what these manual workers thought about differences between types of pubs. Were there different types of pubs?

Ted was very forthcoming. 'There are posh pubs but I don't think' em middle class. I know this is a rough pub. Lots of crap going round. Everybody knows everyone else and knows who's boss. You've got the hard ones, the ones you joke with, the nasty ones, quiet ones, a rough pub is one where everyone knows everyone else. You've got king men who take the piss out of you and take you out, and women nearly all the same. Any women in this pub offers herself. Take slag Susan, she's got a tough boyfriend who doesn't mind who she goes to bed with. You don't want to be in his bed when he gets home. Jesus, I wouldn't mix with her. Middle-class people go to pubs - not this one but some others I bike to. You'll tell 'em by them bringing friends, middle-class people come together an' don't mix. I go to different pubs. '

Russell offered: 'Certainly, yes there are different kinds of pubs. There are some pubs I wouldn't like my wife to go to. Well, there's no point in naming pubs, there's a lot of pubs that are - I wouldn't say working class 'cos I'm working class me-self - get people in that drink from lunchtime to closing time and that's it, there are hard drinking pubs and they can be anywhere. Yes, you know, there aren't distinct border lines but I think there are different kinds of pub. I like a pub I can relax in and not worry about who's stood behind me, and about my wife being with me and things like that, you know, the type of people in some pubs are the type of people it's best not to know, you know, and obviously you must catorgorise them because that type of person wouldn't be served in the place I go to. There are some people if they get a beer in them they have got to throw something about, or whatever you know, unfortunately there are that type of person and they do get known around the pubs, and there are certain pubs they're OK and certain pubs that they aren't. They go where they can get served.'

Clive commented: 'Some pubs you go in and everybody is looking at you, they watch you and see what you do as much as to say, "what are you doing here?" No there aren't middle-class and working-class pubs. There are some that accept folk as however they want to go in, whether they are mucked, clean or however they are. There's obviously ones that accept you only if you're dressed up or whatever, but there's no middle class.'

Both Terry and Brian thought there were different types of pubs and where they were situated - town centre or suburb - had much to do with the type of pub they were, but they were also directly influenced by who used them.

Terry said: 'There are different types of pubs and you'll tell 'em with the regular people that go in - if you went there often enough you'd find out. I think especially in a town centre place there are certain people who when they'd had some beer get violent - they cause trouble. There are I should say respectable pubs and rough pubs, not working and middle class -then a bit of both, mixed I should say.'

Brian responded positively: 'Definitely there are different types of pubs, I was brought up in Hull in East Yorkshire where there were various grades, several different grades there. Basically you've got the dockside type of pub which is usually a very scruffy place, not many amenities, frequented by sailors and prostitutes. Then as you go into the centre of the town you get the type of pub that is frequented by business people - very full at lunchtime between llam and 3pm, but in the evening they're dead, and then as you move to the outskirts of the city you do get a better class of establishment - mostly pubs that have been built in the last twenty years. You get some very very nice pubs. You could take anybody to them. Definitely there are working-class and middle- class pubs. I know a pub called the Volunteers - I've been in it once and that was too much. Pig and Pigeon I'd call it. If you go into the Volunteers you can always smell the disinfectant and that puts you off to start with, it's like going into a clinic.'

Tommy was his usual graphic self: 'Well, you've got lots of pubs to suit kids, them looking for a joggle, then there's the bleeding nobs' places where's them's looks down on you. This is my sort of pub, it's the best place to drink with your mates, I come in as I like, don't know how you got in! How about another pint?'

Some of the other respondents were much less certain. John who was fifty eight, a joiner with two grown up children, and a regular at the Nelson: said, 'Pubs are mainly mixed nowadays, it's better that way'. Another Nelson regular was Ken, aged forty three, a construction worker with one child, who suggested that what mattered to him was the differences between pubs which were like barns - cold places, and small cosy pubs which were small and warm -like the Nelson.

What can be sustained from the less well off, is that there are two different types of pubs, that the rough pub is certainly distinguished by its clients, hard male drinkers characterised by tough masculine values - 'balls over brains' as the rough customers would put it. The mixed pub, in our typology known as the respectable working-class pub, is recognised. The existence of a posh pub seems in doubt, certainly from the regulars' perspective - but we have not interviewed the women or the middle-class participants thus perhaps we will not make a judgement yet. The preliminary conclusions seem to support our theoretical typology in the previous chapters. The key in the rough pub appears to be the link between heavy drinking among men and a hierarchical organisation of the pub dependent upon 'king men who can take you out'. What appears to be crucial is the role of the publican as suggested by Russell, and the factors identified by Brian and Terry, a tendency for the locational factors to be a predisposition for some social groups rather than others and in some ways rather than others.

A third factor is one of the probing of how the regulars regard the changes which they have experienced in the types of pubs - in the improved public house provision. The customers did express a wide variation in their knowledge, and on reflection it did seem optimistic. However Brian, who was old enough to remember the changes observed: 'In your old days you'd have your select room if you were out with your girlfriend you would take her to what was known as the snug, which was a nice cosy room where you could have a pleasant chat, plus which you got waiter service. The old waiter service is gone now. While you used to pay a penny for that privilege. Well, OK it was only a penny on a drink - it was the service I liked. You didn't have to queue up at the bar and things life that. Yes, you did get a different sort of people using the same pub - you'd get the cloth capped type in the taproom - there'd be no carpet on the floor, scrubbed wooden floors with scrubbed wooden tables, and no amenities whatsoever and usually wooden benches all around the walls. But then again, you used to go into the lounge bar - the clerical type would go in there and so in actual fact, in those days you could separate your pub off into different people in different rooms. Now of course you can't. I've known people change their pubs, when a certain pub was modernised and the taproom changed and that was their domain, so they stopped drinking there and went to another pub which had a taproom'. Brian also thought that the brewers had a deliberate strategy to make the pub a more 'middle-class type of establishment'.

Russell said: 'Yes, I think they changed quite a lot. Obviously inside they've changed and because a lot of pubs have been altered and modernised you know, I mean a pub used to have a smoke or tap room, whatever, now they are more open plan. I think the changes are good in a way, you know, there's more variation of pubs' you know, more variation where you can go. Though I think I prefer things as they are. Going back, a woman can go into quite a few pubs on her own and feel at ease whereas at one time she couldn't you know'.

Terry had some observations, 'The atmosphere changed. I think there's more people under age than when I was eighteen, it didn't happen the same, they don't bother now. There's young lasses going in at fourteen, they look eighteen. Don't like new style pubs myself, prefer it how it used to be with your taproom and lounge. Some pubs haven't changed, they're the same.'

Ted from the Fox and Hounds said: 'There isn't as many. Lots of people go to one and then stop. I can't do with small rooms, I like to see everybody in the pub.' Whereas Tommy wished they would 'stop fucking about with pubs', he preferred them as they used to be and said he would 'go miles' to his sort of pub.

A scrutiny of the kinds of changes experienced suggests a stealth strategy was being wrought by licensing justices and breweries so that the new consumers would be young and classless. In the Post War period the breweries have tended to rationalise ie close, and improve ie introduce open plan, with design changes having important consequences for the patterns and experiences of drinking. There was a surprising awareness of the changes in pub usage by a younger age group and under-age drinkers, an attempt to make the pub more accessible to women so that they feel 'more at ease', changes in the physical structure of pubs with the possible mix of different social groups. There was also the importance of physical location in Brian's awareness of the changes, but generally the constraints of a 'civilising morality' -which has had the effect of more drinkers but each drinker drinking less, by broadening the appeal of alcohol to young people and women - has been successful.

3. Drinking, Games and Friendship Participation

The male working class interviewed were all questioned about the nature of their public house participation and their particular usage of the public house. Drinking and what it did for participants. The importance of games and to assess whether the friendship was pub focused or not, are examined. These issues are the famous 'focal interests' and should be considered with the reasons given earlier for going to the pub.

All the male manual workers interviewed were beer drinkers, none would not go to any particular pub because of the drink sold, except Terry who could not 'take' Tetleys. All drank a large amount on any particular pub visit, concentrating in the evening time - they would consume ten to fifteen pints. The 'Rough pub' customers tended to drink heavily on Thursday, Friday and Saturday, whereas the customers of 'respectable pubs' spread their drinking over the week.

When I asked them why they drink, and what it does for them, many of them portrayed the image conjured up by the Pub and People study, and the experience of a 'mental holiday' pictured by the College of Psychiatry Report. Terry responded: 'A drink relaxes me and I drink a lot out of frustration and boredom. When you're not working you don't look forward to going out at night - with not working I mean. When you're working I mean. When you're working you look forward to going out at night. '

Russell said: 'I like a nice drink, to go out to my local and meet people, you know, I don't go purely for the alcohol, I go for the company. After a day's hard work I like to go to the pub to have a chat and unwind and have a drink and feel at peace with the world, it's nice you know?'

Brian proposed the following: 'Basically I'm a beer drinker. I like beer but the type of beer doesn't influence my going to the Nelson. I use the Nelson a lot because I know everybody that goes in and I meet people in there. Drinking relaxes me, it makes me more sociable. I would say that after three pints I might speak to someone that I wouldn't speak to otherwise.'

Clive said: 'There are some beers I like and some beers I don't but it wouldn't make me go into one pub and not another. I could always get bottled, like it seems more or less the same is bottled. I usually get noisy when I've a few drinks in me, I used to get violent, I don't anymore though, I go the other way. Liz says I get daring when I've had a few drinks. '

Ted volunteered: 'I like bottled Guinness, drinks it all the time. If I've worked hard I like to drink, it relaxes me. Some nights I go out set on getting sloshed. If I'm mad at someone I like to drink too much. I'd talk to anyone after three bottles of Guinness.'

Whereas Tommy said: 'Drink, me drink a lot? Six or seven pints - you 'ave to drink don't yer. Keeps yer going, I mean a man's got to 'ave beer. What's it do for me? Makes me sit 'ere. Makes me forget s'pose. I can forget out there and don't tell me it does 'arm 'cos me father drank all his life and died when he was seventy six. Beer, good stuff.'

Drinking did provide a form of mental holiday, a chance to get out and away from the constraints of work and everyday life, a vital contrasting experience to most of other social experiences. A chance to retreat into being oneself. For many the drinking went along with a form of sociability, to meeting others. talking, celebrating some element of human communality. Tommy and Terry certainly enjoyed drinking and it was a focal interest in contrast to the constraints of work and everything' out there' .

The participation in the games aspect by public-house respondents was very variable indeed. For some it was a highly obsessive interest, such as Terry who offered the following. 'I only play pool. When I go into a pub, I have a look round, see who's in, and put my name down. Winner stays on job. Whoever's in t'pub if they happen to be there I'll say "d'you wanna play?", if they do its good news. I always think I'm gonna win y'see. I'm no good at darts, don't bother with cards, dominoes and machines. I don't like TV's - you come from home to get away from that sort of thing, don't yer? Pool and juke box are important to me, the rest, forget 'em'.

Ted regarded games in pubs as marginal to his participation, thus: 'Don't play games in pubs, don't play gaming machines. TV - no point in coming out, might as well be at home. Juke boxes - I don't put money in them.'

Russell had a similar view: 'Games, doesn't bother me at all. Don't play games, darts or cards or anything like that. I'll have a dabble but I'm not enthusiastic. I'm not bothered. I think TV's OK in centre of pubs for horse racing. Wouldn't stop me going in, wouldn't stop me staying in. Juke boxes. I like them.' Tommy contributed: 'S'pose them'll do fort'kids. Lots of hassle. Makes for fists when sods'll go for a set-to, them's games all over, space invaders and joggling music. Me pub, I likes for me mates and drink. TV, I like the horses and a bit of sport. Don't care if you'll get rid of the fucking lot.'

It was self evident that taking part in the games side of the pub regardless of age was fairly low in the focal interests, even for the young people, of the participants. Most took no interest in the games and at worst would' get rid of the fucking lot'. An attempt was made to uncover the sociability aspect of the public-house life fOf the respondents. 'What do you do when you go into a pub - especially your regular? What do you talk about? How important are jokes and humour? Do you take friends into the pub or do you meet people in here?'

As Terry said: 'I go by myself to a pub - I'm a loner. When I go in, I buy my drink. I have a look round, see who's in. I'm a stander-upper but I might sit down at a table if I have a woman with me. I talk about sport - I'm a football fanatic. Cheers me up. Joking helps yer - as if you're meeting strangers you get talking to them with an acceptable joke. People I meet in the pub are mates.'

Ted ventured: 'Don't take people into pubs. I go to meet my buddies. I stand - I like to be in the middle where I can revolve - don't sit at the bar or at a table. I talk about bikes and bikes - I go around with bikers. I meet my girlfriend in the pub and leave her there. '

Clive said: 'I go by myself but sit with the same crowd every night. No special pattern. It depends on who's in partly but if there is only two of us - me and Liz - we sit us down don't we? We usually split up - she'll want to talk about dressmaking - she can go with her friends and talk about what she wants. If! want to talk about cars or sport I don't go and sit with her friends. I go and sit with mine don't I? People I meet in the pub are mates. I usually stand at the bar for a bit, I talk about work, cars, other people sport, scandal. There are lots of comments in the pub - wisecracks I'd say.'

Russell's contribution was: 'I tend to go by myself during the week, weekends - Saturdays, my wife and I will probably go in together. We'll meet someone we know but we don't go in purely to meet someone we know, we don't arrange anything beforehand. The men, we stand and talk and chat. We sit at the tables with the womenfolk and that, but you know, we'll stand at the bar and chat with the publican. People I meet in the pub - mates, but I take friends in too with my wife. If I go by myself I inevitably stand at the bar. I talk about work, women, but I aren't into politics and things like that. I'm argumentative so I don't like to get into differences that way, just general things really. Joking - yes the pub wouldn't be the same without a good joke, y'know.'

Brian suggested: 'I usually go by myself and meet people in the pub, sometimes its prearranged but usually not. If I'm by myself I tend to stand at the bar, there's always the chance of an intelligent conversation. It's a bit of a habit to lean against the bar, with luck I could even talk to a good-looking barmaid. I don't take in people I work with or live near. Jokes - personally I'm a bit of an introvert person, I don't like the rowdy type of company where everybody is laughing their heads off. I like a good joke and usually talk about things of the moment. I suppose people I meet - not friends perhaps mates or maybe acquaintances.'

Tommy responded: 'I bring me self in and stand up at the front. I see all the pub and am with me mates keeps ovver fuckers away. Jokes - jokers we take out when we have to. Talks about all sorts - making a bit, doing jobs, horses, all sorts. '

What is important about such responses is the extent the public house was used for socially meeting other people - people by and large 'accidentally' in the pub, with no arrangement which was fixed beforehand. If one thinks across institutions in contemporary society it is difficult to envisage others where there is such an expectation without an outcome. It was an outcome in itself. What is also important is that it is the maleness of such comments, where men are mates, where womenfolk sit at tables and men stand at the bar. Is it coercion or is it choice one must ask. The public house is a snapshot of social reality which is portrayed as a social context of male values with women present but in a parallel rather than a shared social world. It is thus to the explicit maleness of such contexts that attention now turns.

4. Men's Views of Women's Participation in Pubs

All of the regulars I interviewed thought that, on average, the ratio of women to men in pubs was between three and four men to every one woman. However it depended on the pub concerned, and what time of the day and what night of the week I was talking about. Pubs in the centre of town, and more generally at lunchtime, could have a much higher ratio of women. They also proposed that the ratio on Friday and Saturday nights was higher as they were traditional nights for couples going out, and people going out generally after a week of work. Although they did not think that women played as many games - such as pool or space invaders - as men they expressed no strong objections to women playing such games or to women's teams. They were less sure about mixed teams, mainly because women did not take the game as seriously as men and were usually relatively unskilled at it. Ted said: 'Women's teams are never up to scratch', whilst Terry said: 'I've never seen a good women pool player yet, I can't see it because women as a rule wouldn't stand a chance, they don't take it as serious.' These were typical comments. What I was particularly interested in however was the gender basis - what did they see as the attitudes of women as individuals and groups in pubs?

Women by themselves or in groups were perceived by the working-class men as basically hostile or available in the pub. In asking these questions they were put quite impartially. Ted said: 'Women who go in on their own are out for what they can get, they're on the pick-up', and Terry said: 'I ask what they are doing by themselves, I try to chat them up but don't often get far. Some women like getting picked up. If I see a woman at the bar, she's fair game.' Tommy said: 'Women, what's on them's own? Fucking cows.' Less unsophisticated, but equally unambiguous was Brian: 'Women in pubs, I don't think a lot to it. Where a man will go in on his own, a woman in a pub - well, she's either waiting for someone or she's available. I usually wait half an hour or so to see. After two or three pints a man can let his imagination run away with him. A man will automatically think, ah, this one's on the loose.'

All of the men who were working-class regulars answered the questions about the place of women. All the pub regulars saw the pub as a man's world and perceived and acted upon the sexual stereotyping of women. The public house as a social context in which women, if they were unescorted or without a male companion, certainly were sexually available ie, they were 'fair game', or 'fucking cows'. Such a view of women on their own in pubs was very pervasive indeed among the male manual workers. The only real exception was Russell who said he rather liked to see women in pubs, 'Its a sign that things are changing, you know, perhaps in the past women have been afraid to come into pubs, but I like to see it, you know'. By and large, after a few pints, a man would let his 'imagination run away with him', and for all the manual pub regulars they shared a similar view, that it is exceptional to find women by themselves in pubs, coming in alone into such a context, and if they did, it was assumed that they were waiting for someone, not that they had the right to be there on their own to relax and drink - unlike men who could come in and have any extreme excuse for participation. The strength and pervasiveness of such an attitude was considerable - any women alone in a pub was offering herself. How influential was drinking in the process and how much did women share the view? We will leave such questions to the later analysis.

5. The Publican in the Working-Class Pubs

The final probing of the attitudes of the male manual workers to the pub focused on the publican's role. They were asked about what they thought about the length of the publican's working week? What makes for a good publican? Could they distinguish between the tenant and the manager, and if they themselves would like to be a publican? They themselves argued that the publican's role could be an arduous one with long and unusual hours of work - but it depended upon whether the landlord had 'help', whether he 'did meals', and in general what sort of pub he ran, ie the number and type of people who used it.

Terry observed: 'A good landlord can make all the difference in the world because there are certain pubs where I hate the landlord.'

Clive said: 'The landlord makes a lot of difference, he's got to concentrate on everybody without concentrating on me. Not treat everybody equal, but not stick to one all night. '

Ted said: 'Important, yeah. I like the ones that talk to you, not sarcastic sods.'

Tommy claimed that the 'landlord - got to be important. He's with the lad's, 'as to be one of us'.

Russell said: 'Yes he is important. He has to have a bit of personality. He doesn't have to come beaming over his face every time you come in, you know. But he is important. I've spoken to people when a pub changed hands and they'll say, it's not the same as it used to be, I'm not gonna go in there again - it can be the guy who's changed it.'

Brian said: 'Makes or breaks it doesn't he. He has to be a public relations officer and a diplomat - look after the beer and the customers.'

Those interviewed were asked what were the most important things about a good publican or landlord and any differences in their own experience between tenants and managers.

Ted said: 'I like a landlord who comes out from behind the bar, like this one, he's with us. He has to keep his pub so you're not falling over his stuff, and with plenty of room for people to stand. Tenants are more sociable, and the only manager I know doesn't like us bikers going to his pub. If a bloke owns a place he'll risk after-hours drinking more.'

Ken said: 'A good landlord? Being fair with customers, like somebody who comes to the bar first should get served first. He has to be one of the lads, obviously some might not like it. Managers won't be bothered whether he's taking much at the till or not will he? Whereas a proper landlord will take as much as he can.'

Clive suggested the following: 'Somebody who appreciates us customers and doesn't take us for granted. Sometimes he gets a bit much - you have to serve yourself. I like the atmosphere he creates, his character. He's got to talk to everyone. Managers don't joke with customers, not usually and if you've had a bit and its after time won't serve you, a bloke who owns a place would say, have a bottle.'

Russell said: 'Personality counts a lot, its nice to be made welcome in a pub, I don't expect him to bow to me, but say "good evening" you know, rather than throw the dishcloth in the sink and say "what do you want". I like a clean pub and good beer and somewhere I can take my wife on Saturdays. I don't think managers are the same as tenants - it's more of a tenant's own place. It's success depends a large amount on him, you know. '

Brian flourished the following: 'The publican has got to be pleasant with regard to customers. Even if! only buy one pint I expect him to say "good evening" and "goodbye". He must keep good beer and keep the place clean. I like a publican who can hold an intelligent conversation. Some can manage it and some can't. Managers and tenants are different in their attitudes. The manager is paid a salary at the end of the week, he doesn't in my estimation take as much care of his pub. You will find that most city centre-pubs are managed, they have become dispensing establishments with no atmosphere. I think managers are less inclined to get on with people, they always close on time. He doesn't have to go out of his way to attract a person to come back to that pub, you see, because he couldn't care less really, for instance, if a landlord upsets three or four of his best customers, seven nights a week drinkers, he's lost a lot of money, so he doesn't do this. A manager couldn't care less.'

Tommy said: 'A landlord - this one? He's one of us, helps us out, gives us a lift, a good 'un. Managers - don't trust em, them's couldn't give a shit.'

Several important elements present themselves. What mattered to the regular male working-class participants was above the social nature of the publican or landlord - they would support him being a participant, rather than a dispenser of drinks or an observer. He was one of the lads rather than a situational policeman. The regulars thought it more likely that tenants than managers could be trusted, he was one of them, he was more likely to serve drinks after hours, and generally related to his customers. They all suggested that he was a central factor in making the pub 'happen', he 'makes it or breaks it'. Was the publican the key to understanding the pub? Was it a combining of the regulars and the publicans needs so that together they became deregulated or perhaps that the pub becomes a refuge of timeless behaviour. Given that publicans have such a high level of drinking, it may well be the case. It may also be the case that the combination of heavy drinking, a sense of ego attraction and the escape from the onerous demands of work and family, are irresistible. As we shall see there are very different views expressed by the male middle class public-house users, to which we now turn.

Chapter 10

Talking with the Middle Class About Their Participation

Middle-class men who used the posh Sutcliffe Arms visited the pub once or twice a month, invariably drove, spread their usage over the days of the week, and appeared to fit in going to the public house with business and friendship schedules. They also tended to take a partner or friend with them - a factor which emerges as a salient feature of their pub usage. One other factor, they tended to go to one pub and stay, rather than go around the pubs in a pub-hopping session.

Michael, aged forty seven, a personnel director, married with two children twelve and fifteen, and a regular at the Sutcliffe Arms said: 'I drive to the nearest pub - what is it called? yes that's right, The Sutcliffe Arms. I visit it once or twice a month, mainly in the evenings. When I go depends on what I am going out for. Usually we go out as a couple, or with friends and it might be on the way out for a meal or to visit people we know.'

Richard aged thirty four, married with one child aged seven and regular at the Sutcliffe Arms, said: 'I tend to go to different pubs at different times for different reasons. It's a natural place to take customers to lunch, that or restaurants. My evening use of the Sutcliffe Arms is fairly patchy. My work takes precedence and I am away from home quite a lot but when I am home I go to the pub about twice a month - usually with friends, sometimes with people I work with.'

Graham, fifty four, a bank manager with two teenage children and regular at the Sutcliffe Arms said: 'I suspect I'm not the best person to interview about pubs. I don't really approve of drinking for its own sake. I do go to the pub, maybe about once a month. It's about a mile and a half - I always drive because I'm not going to consume much, usually. If we go in a group - with friends - one of us will decide to drive for the evening. My wife can drive so there is no difficulty about that. I never visit a pub during the day and rarely during the week, its a Saturday or Sunday evening usually. For some people I know the pub is a way of life.'

Steven aged twenty seven, married, no children, an educational psychologist
Graham, fifty four, a bank manager with two teenage children and regular at the Sutcliffe Arms said: 'I suspect I'm not the best person to interview about pubs. I don't really approve of drinking for its own sake. I do go to the pub,

maybe about once a month. It's about a mile and a half - I always drive because I'm not going to consume much, usually. If we go in a group - with friends - one of us will decide to drive for the evening. My wife can drive so there is no difficulty about that. I never visit a pub during the day and rarely during the week, its a Saturday or Sunday evening usually. For some people I know the pub is a way of life.'

Steven aged twenty seven, married, no children, an educational psychologist and a regular at the Nelson said: 'I do drive to my local but really prefer to walk - it seems much more civilised to walk. I go to a pub perhaps three or four times a month, occasionally for sustenance. It makes a nice beginning to the evening if we are going on somewhere, or else we might visit for the last hour or so to round off a night out.'

David aged twenty four, a teacher, married with one child, a regular to the Nelson, said: 'I go on average once a month, usually 1 drive. I don't go to drink although I do enjoy a good pint of beer. I suppose I go more often than not because it's a nice place to take friends or guests.'

What is interesting about these men is the infrequency with which they visited the pub. It was a much less frequent activity than it was for the other workingclass manual workers interviewed. Also it is clear that they rarely went by themselves - they went with wives or friends, and not only that, but used the pub as incidental to their other arrangements and plans.

1. Why They Visited the Pub and Types of Pub

The same approach was used as with the other people interviewed, they were asked for the three reasons why they went to the pub - to be listed in any order of importance.

Richard said: 'I come to get work out of my mind, also I enjoy a pint relaxation is the prime motivation. '

David said: 'To go with someone 1 haven't seen for a while - generally taking them with me. The three most important reasons? Relaxation, I suppose good beer, but perhaps for me privacy is the most important reason. '

Michael said: 'To be together with friends or a colleague, to have a drink although I can always have a drink at home, 1 can't think of a third - we like dining out and the Sutcliffe Arms does serve a passable meal so perhaps that's the third reason. '

None of the men interviewed - nine in all- ever mentioned the reason that was the most important for the first group of men, meeting mates or known others in the pub. Nor did they see the public house as an important drinking context. At most they would have two or three pints or two or three shorts, and were aware of the 'drinking and driving' problem - five of the nine mentioned this.

What however seemed to dominate their usage of the pub, the reasons why they went at all, was a convenient place to take friends and relax - certainly a place in which to relax from work, but not with just anybody their friends, their partner from home, their colleague from work.

As with the manual workers, these non-manual pub participants were asked whether there are different kinds of pubs and how they have changed. Like the manual workers they had fairly unambiguous views.

Richard said: 'Yes, you've got your spitoon and sawdust type - rather reminiscent of the small run-down pubs, mainly in what I suppose one would term working-class localities. They are pretty ghastly some of them. I've been in them. Rough pubs, yes, I should say so. Depends on who goes in them doesn't it. '

David said: 'I suppose there could well be, but I'm not really sure. Pubs I suspect do have different clientele and reputation. I wouldn't be worried about going into a pub with a reputation but I might well not like what goes on inside it. I don't suppose pubs set out to be different types but who uses them pushes them in a particular direction. I suspect that it might have a lot to do with the licensee. '

Steven observed: 'There are what I would call working-class and bar-lounge type pubs - pubs are very much class distinguishable. You can tell the difference by the clientele, the decor and the friendliness. Working-class pubs are far friendlier than the bar-lounge type. I suppose it's because such pubs tend to be small, the bar is the main feature, seating is minimal and consequently you are likely to stand at the bar and that encourages social intercourse. In the bar-lounge type the seating arrangements I think, encourages social distance.

Kevin aged twenty one, a bank clerk, unmarried and a regular at the Sutcliffe Arms, said: 'Pubs have different atmospheres - some are cold, large and impersonal, with the landlord who serves you a pint and goes away. Others are bright and warm with a friendly landlord. I suppose there are rough pubs but that's a bit outside my experience I'm afraid.'

Michael said: 'Some pubs I wouldn't stop at. If they don't serve meals or if they don't offer some privacy where I can sit and chat, I have no use for them. There are different types of pubs - I try and go to what one would call the better class of pub - places where you don't get the yobs and the toughies - the leather-jacket boys.'

Such comments perhaps reveal as sharp a range of conceptions of the pub as among the manual workers in the previous chapter. What was most interesting was the differences between pubs for them - pubs that served meals, the bar-lounge type, the avoidance of yobs and toughies, the assertion that the clientele 'make' the pub. Some pubs were pretty ghastly, others offered privacy and encouraged social distance.

The third area pursued was how the pubs have changes and are changing. Generally there was a recognition that such changes have occurred and some of the critical comments were forthcoming about some of the trends.

David said: 'My experience is limited but my impression is that they have changed in terms of women being accepted into the life of the pub. More pubs now provide food and entertainment - pool and fruit machines. Pubs have of course been opened up and the taproom people have as it were been abolished in the process. I think it good that there should be both sorts of pubs - pubs with little rooms where you can talk without piped music bellowing through, and pubs which are more open plan with everything open to view as it were. I suppose the advantage of the open plan pub is that one doesn't have people stepping out of acceptable bounds of behaviour. '

Steven responded: 'Pubs have changed and not all the changes are for the better. The range and quality of beer has deteriorated and I think that electronic equipment has changed the clientele. Brewers have a conception of comfortable living which they have foisted on the drinking public - creating plastic, artificial and pretentious environments. I am ambivalent about open plan pubs, in theory they ought to lead to a classless clientele with a bar lounge atmosphere which discourages the working man in his overalls. In practice I don't think such trends are successful in breaking down class barriers. I can see great advantages in the multi-bar pub with cosy friendly atmosphere vis-a-vis bam type places.'

Michael said: 'Pubs have changed, they have become more uniform and I am sure many regulars don't like their pub environment changed. I think choice has been reduced in respect of the different pubs available - they all have juke boxes and machines. There is not much choice any more. Also I think the age level of drinkers in pubs has dropped, there are more young people using them, and it's to suit the younger element that some of the changes have been introduced. '

Richard said: 'Certain changes I have noticed. One can go more often than not and notice a pub which is of a better standard. The old style pubs are going, only slowly I grant you but there is, if you like, an image to live down, the spitoon and sawdust type with men as men chucking beer down their throats as fast as they can go - that's going. Also I think that men are slowly accepting the inevitable, that women have a right to go into pubs - not with some he-man but on a more equal basis. I welcome that for myself. The one change I loathe is the electronic machines - some pubs are like amusement arcades. I basically go to a pub to talk to people - in some you can't hear yourself think. '

Graham responded: 'Yes, pubs have changed. In my boyhood they were on every corner. I had a tough upbringing and where we lived in Birmingham some pretty terrible goings-on occurred in pubs and outside them. There were fights and general rowdiness and it was very much accepted that the pub was a place for men. One sees much less drunkenness now, perhaps it occurs in people's homes rather than in the public house. I like to see the pubs brightened up. Undoubtedly there are still the traditional type of pub but less of them, and that must be a good thing.'

Kevin said: 'I really don't know, I suppose they have changed, but its difficult to pinpoint the changes. I think they've become more open - a greater range of people going into them. '

The impression given by such comments is mixed. The factors mentioned, more women in pubs, more younger men and women, the quality of beer, the installation of machines, the failure of the mixturing of pub clientele, 'improvement' or otherwise of opening-up pub premises. What did impress me about the issues of change were those which concentrated upon the decrease in privacy - the loss of small rooms, the invasion by music or machines to decrease the element of conversation in pubs. The men may have drunk less in the pub, but they were certainly aware of the changes which had occurred.

To a large extent what they drank, and how much, depended upon how long they intended to spend in the pub and whether they intended to have a meal, how far they were driving, and whom they were with. On average these regulars drunk between one and three pints of beer and went into the pub for between half an hour up to two hours either around 7pm or from 9.30pm depending on whom they were with, they would talk about 'personal things. '

Steven said that it covered 'like what to do about the rain pouring through the roof at home or the logistics about managing the company finances for next month'.

Or as David commented: 'Well, I go into the pub, buy my drink, usually a pint of bitter, I'm not a great peanut or crisp fan, I sit down and talk. As I usually go with friends, or those I've prearranged to meet, I've made my choice of conversation before I go, and that's different to just going into a pub and someone starts talking to you that you don't know. The type of beer is not important to me, I quite like the flavour, after working it helps one to relax, that's about all. I'm not perceptibly more sociable after two pints or so - at least not to myself. '

Drinking was not the dominant focal interest although it was an important ingredient in the leisure and relaxation offered by the pub. Richard said: 'After a drink I am more relaxed. I know it probably is a combination effect company I enjoy being with, a slight loss of inhibitions, a feeling of being able to forget interests and mortgages - and of course work.'

Michael pointed to the following: 'I think it makes a person seem more intelligent to themselves whilst becoming less coherent to others - which isn't so bad if you're all becoming less coherent at the same time.'

As already indicated the respondents generally did not drink a great deal at the pub itself, although they did indicate that there were occasions when they were glad they had not been breathalysed.

The games element for the middle-class respondents varied from mild disinterest to open hostility. Kevin said: 'I don't play games in pubs - very rarely anyway. It's just not my thing. I don't go to the pub for that'.

Richard said: 'I don't use the games facilities - 95% of the time they don't matter. The TV is not synonymous with the pub for me - its rather like the jukebox only more so, it's intrusive. If we've gone to the pub for dinner then we might play pool - to round off the evening'.

Michael said: 'I don't object to the games element in the pub - some people like playing these things. As for myself! go to relax, to get away from people and just like to sit and chat.'

David answered the question on games in pubs, 'I go to the pub with friends - sometimes I play pool. I can watch TV at home. Jukeboxes - yes I like background music but not too loud. I can take or leave one armed bandits. I might put 20p in on the way out. Games aren't that important - they wouldn't influence whether I went to a pub - I don't think I would miss them although I like to think myself good at pool- although I am usually not.'

Graham said: 'Games - what games? No I can't stand them.'

There was little difference in the age of those who pursued games - virtually none of them did nor wished to do so. They might play pool now and again with friends. Games and entertainment aspects were low on the scale of focal interests for manual workers, they were virtually nonexistent for those interviewed at the posh pub who were in various non-manual occupations.

What of friendship and how was it expressed in relation to the pub? It was fairly clear that friendship assumed a very high priority but it was of a very different kind to that involved in the rough and respectable pub members. They did not go to meet' mates', 'I don't have any mates in the pub, sounds a rather strange category, I don't think I have mates, some acquaintances perhaps. No I don't go to see the people there', says Richard. Another, Michael said: 'I suppose one could meet people in the pub and find a common interest but this is quite rare in my experience. I don't expect that from a public house. The people I go with are quite important people for me. We sit and chat about the sorts of things which keep friendship alive, perhaps work and the economic situation generally, perhaps our families. I don't expect to strike up casual relationships. I think that there is a male/female difference here. If we go with another couple I usually fnd myself spending my time talking to the male partner - even if! do find his wife attractive. It rather depends whose friends they are - my wife's or mine.'

Kevin claimed: 'I find it quite difficult to meet peop.~~in the pub - other than on a superficial level. I usually find that I have little in common with them. It's easy enough to be on a nodding acquaintance I suppose but I'd hardly call that being mates, would you?'

Steven said: 'Pubs aren't usually places I meet people, they are places I take people to. I find other people stimulating but really I have enough of meeting people I don't know in my professional role - I want to be with others in a group situation but be able to distance myself from them. '

The middle-class pub regulars regarded the pub almost as a service station compared to the working class who saw it as another home. The purpose was not to meet 'mates' , not regard it as a place to drink, not to regard it as a world in itself. It was rather a place to relax, get work out of their minds, to bring their friends into the pub, to juggle their commitments to work, family and leisure. The public house was not a locus around which other things occurred and around which other relationships were centred. The middle class used the pub as a context for private interaction, not drinking very much, not playing games, and above all not readily available for casual encounters. It was a public situation of private interaction, whereas in the Nelson and the Fox and Hounds it was a private situation of public interaction. Was it the little alcohol consumed, was it the attitude of the publican, was it a much increased presence of women which changed the situation? We shall see.

3. Men and Women in the Pub

The claims made by the men in the Sutcliffe Arms was a small sample of the total of those who go as regulars to similar types of pubs. It is only small but some care is taken as the views of the men are prescribed. I personally view the findings as the men adopting an attitude of paternalistic egalitarianism, but judge for yourselves.

The male pub regulars estimated that the ratio of women using pubs was 3:2 but that ratio could vary very much depending upon the time of day and location of the pub - city-centre pubs at lunchtime tended to contain a much higher proportion of women than local pubs in the evening. They thought that women drank as much in terms of alcohol- but in shorts rather than in pints.

Steven said about women in pubs: 'I try to adopt an encouraging attitude. Women essentially don't like pubs and feel they are tolerated because they have a male escort. For many women the pub is historically men's domain. They find it an anxiety provoking situation and often don't like going into a pub by themselves to meet someone they have prearranged to meet. I strongly suspect that the very act of going into a traditional male preserve, unaccompanied, is a signal which says "I'm available", and could lead to an embarrassing situation. I don't think if pubs were open all day - as they are now - more women would go into them. For women coming into a pub and being at the bar signals availability for social intercourse - or the other kind of intercourse.'

David was more concerned with the family responsibilities of women. 'If I see a women by herself in a pub I think she's probably waiting to meet someone. I haven't any objection to women in pubs providing other responsibilities are taken care of - I wouldn't want to see children on the streets or neglected. From my own experience of women I'm acquainted with, most won't go into a pub on their own. They might not know anyone or they may think it says something about them as a person. Also, the pub is more of an after work phenomenon and therefore its a question of going out in the dark and you wouldn't expect to see women wandering around by themselves after dark no more than in parks or other places of recreation.'

Michael had some concern for women, 'I like to have women in pubs but, you know it's still a man's world, even though women have more money and more independence, they are still not as socially accepted in the pub as in most other public places. '

Graham said for him it was a question of the stigma which resulted from going to pubs. 'I think there is still something of a stigma, at least in the minds of women themselves, about going into a pub just to have a drink. The brewers have tried very hard to encourage them, by providing meals, better decor and by making drinking more socially acceptable, but there is something I personally find objectionable about seeing a woman propping up the bar. I think that if she's socially prepared to talk to anyone it does have sexual overtones.'

Richard made clear the repression of men by the women's admission to the pub, 'Women by themselves? I like to see them in pubs. It's a much more -socially healthy situation: Jt.means that a lot of the excesses of men by themselves are restrained - bad language and irresponsible behaviour in particular', whilst Kevin simply stated that: 'Women are as likely to go in pubs as men nowadays but I think nothing to it. '

These men interviewed were very aware of the sexual stereotyping of women in pubs, that it could be an embarrassing situation and sexually threatening especially for women by themselves. If a woman was alone in a pub she was waiting for somebody. None of the men concerned were so explicit as to say that any woman who goes into a pub 'offers herself' but the implicit assumption was that this could be so - particularly with the public house as a traditional male dominated context. One wonders what it would be like in a female domain, would men be happy? They strongly held to the view that, as Michael suggested: 'The pub is a male dominated world even though you will find a 50:50 situation', and as Richard suggested: 'The woman in a pub alone is in a man's world. The pub performs different functions for men and women. It's a place where men can be together - at least traditionally. Women perhaps don't need such a place, but then again, perhaps they are beginning to realise what they have been missing. I like women in pubs but I'd hate it to be a women's world. '

The Publican's Role

The comments by the men in the middle-class public house revealed exactly how they used it. Whether the publican was there or not made little difference. They could not tell the difference between a tenanted or managed pub. They regarded the publican as contributing only a nominal position in front of the bar - nothing more than serving good beer, good food and a pleasant environment - and he only worked an average 60 hours a week - so the regulars estimated. The following are some of the responses elicited.

As David observed: 'I suppose the publican must make a difference, presumably the pub reflects the licensees personality over the years. It doesn't make any difference to me what the landlord is like, I wouldn't necessarily know whether the licensee was there or not, because there will be other people serving behind the bar. A good publican I suppose is one who keeps his beer in good condition, runs a hygienic establishment and can offer food in some form. I don't know enough to comment about any differences between managers and tenants. No, I wouldn't like to be a publican. '

Steven said: 'It really depends on the pub - a lot of casual trade would presumably mean that the publican would play less of a sociable role. It doesn't matter too much to me. I don't need a friendly licensee who greets me with an effusive welcome every time I go in. What I look for is good food and clean beer. I know that there are differences in principle between tenants and managers but in my experience thefe is a lot of mythology about the differences. I do find it difficult to distinguish between them. No, I wouldn't like to be a publican - it's too extensive in terms of lifestyles.'

Michael commented: 'Yes, he can make a difference. He can impress his own style on the pub. I don't look for that however and perhaps I would find it difficult to pick out the publican unless I was very familiar with the pub. As long as I receive pleasant and efficient service I don't worry too much. I like to be known in the pub but I like to be left alone, not that I'm antisocial you understand but I do expect to go into my local pub and give my attention to whoever I'm with.'

Richard said: 'The publican - well I do like to be noticed, at least when I come in, but then I like to merge into the background - I go to the pub I think rather to retreat from people. It sounds rather strange I know but that's how I see it. Whether it's a tenant or a manager doesn't make a big difference - if its a pleasant atmosphere, with reasonable food and beer. I don't ask for much more. Be a publican? Never - I like my leisure. '

Graham offers the final comments made by the men at the Sutcliffe Arms middle-class pub. Graham suggests in response to the questions about the publican: 'The publican - well I do like to be noticed - I am not sure how important he is. In some pubs he might be important. He can be a useful source of information providing he's discreet about his confidences. I think I would know the difference between a manager and a tenant, but if you're asking me whether it makes any difference to my use of the pub - I think not. I want a pub to be a place where I can take people, I don't expect too much help from the publican. No, I wouldn't want a publican's life.'

Several conclusions emerge from these comments by the male users of the middle-class public house. Firstly none of the regulars viewed the publican as a central figure in their social usage of the public house. They wanted him to be pleasant, efficient, serve reasonable beer and food and provide a context they could use for talking and drinking with their friends. They took their own friends to the pub according to their own time schedule. The pub was a segment, but only a segment, of their own social reality. But the way they related to the pub was in complete contrast to the working-class men who met their mates in the pub according to a fixed time schedule - a somewhat complete and immersive way of life. Both groups of men were glad to escape from work and the time constraints of paid employment - the impersonal pressure of social relationships. They resorted to the public house, in the former as an escape into the privacy and privateness of a private world, in the latter as a public world of activity, meeting the lads, and expecting the publican to be one of them.

Chapter 11

Women in the Public House the Gender Class

A woman in a pub alone is 'vulnerable', according to the rough pub men, whereas with respectable pub men they saw her as 'fair game', fier 'waiting for a friend'. Even in the posh pub the view that sexual equality was an ideal for women, but was not achievable, all point to the physical, emotional and cultural dangers for women alone in the public house. As one man in the Sutcliffe Arms put it, the link between social encounters and sexual encounters is very close. So how do women view themselves in relation to the pub and men? Are they free to relate their social freedom to sexual encounters? Do women seek such freedom? Do women 'assume the conventional notion is that because men are continually manufacturing sperm they constantly accumulate sexual tensions which generate an endless succession of intrusive erotic fantasies which become more intensive until some action is performed to dispel them. This pseudo-physiological explanation of masculine genital obsession is simply an excuse for men to deliberate entertainment of fantasies which they endlessly elaborate in search of more effective stimuli. Men work on their fantasies, growing them on a more sumptuous diet of pornography in every available medium.' (I) Rather than disappear into an elaborate miriad of gender differences, the attempt is made to derive from interviews with the women themselves - not about some theory a woman may have about what men think of women - what they have to say is important, without being overlaid by suspicion, doubt, sexual and political inference, and psychological pro-feminist rhetoric.

What is there to prevent women speaking for themselves, of saying what they think and believe, being the way forward in the unknown and uncertain adventure which both women and men share - and the pub is a distinctly unique institution. The women who shared with men in the pubs were generally less knowledgeable, more ambivalent, and are put together in terms of questions answered, comparison within each question on a class basis.

Pub Usage

Sandra a part-time factory packer, married with three children under ten and a regular in the Fox and Hounds. She said: 'I go with me husband on Friday or Saturdays. If we go out on Saturdays it's to the local, Fridays, no if we go out, it's somewhere different. We walk to the local- it's just down the road - but drive to other places. Ifl goes out during the week I goes to me friend's place, not to the pub.' Joan, a shop assistant, unmarried and a regular at the Nelson, said: 'I go out at weekends, Saturday evenings, I do walk but usually get a bus and walk back. It's a bit of a ritual.'

The working-class regulars visited the pub at weekends, or occasionally at Friday at lunchtime. Such a pattern of pub visiting contrasted with the middleclass respondents. Lynne who was forty six, a deputy catering manager, twice married, with three grown-up children and a regular at the Sutcliffe Arms said: 'I go about once a month to the pub, but don't always go to the same pub - it depends upon who I'm with. 1 drive and how long I stay depends on the occasion.' Ann who was thirty two, a contract supervisor, married without children, was quite expansive in her answer. 'I visit the pub about once a month. 1 don't think of a pub as a local. 1 live quite close to the Sutcliffe Arms, it has a nice ambience. You don't get examined as you go through the door, its anonymous enough so that there are no special places that you're not allowed to sit, not too many yobs, the landlord is very nice and there's not too much music, and a nice level of conversation. I'm never going to feel uncomfortable with a fight starting. 1 drive to the Sutcliffe Arms and usually visit before going on somewhere - a dinner party or theatre or something like that. Occasionally I have so many people staying that we want to talk and have a drink.'

The other women had similar usage patterns -less frequent visits to the pub and spending much less time there than their working-class counterparts, using it not so much for a night out, as a convenient location before' going on', or if they were with friends, going out for the evening. The working-class women on the other hand had a much less casual and individualised pattern of usage - they would normally go on a Friday or Saturday after 8pm until closing time, either with their spouse or boyfriend - often meeting the boyfriend in the pub itself, but knowing that other girlfriends would be there.

Types of Pub and the Changes in the Pubs

Why the women went to the pub was interesting. The differences between the groups was both class related and age variable. The working-class women who were unmarried and without a family went predominantly to be with their friends, often keeping in contact with those whom they had known from their schooldays. Meeting the 'girls' seemed to be quite important as an aspect of going to the pub. They did not regard friends as mates - both groups of women rejected the term. They also rejected the term 'pals' but accepted the term 'friends' to apply to the people they knew and either met in, or took to the pub. The working-class women, Freda and Joan were reminiscent to Ted and Clive reported earlier.

Joan said: 'I suppose I go partly to get out of the house. Saturday is a sort of special night, you know after a week's work and watching telly, I like to dress up a bit and go somewhere. My boyfriend and me usually see the people we know, he likes his beer, my meeting the girls I catch up on the gossip. I don't go for the drink, you can get that anywhere.'

Freda said: 'You know, I go 'cos it's a habit, you know, meeting the girls. I might meet a nice fella - mine's alright, but a change is as good as a rest! What else? I quite like to have a drink, warms me up - both ways, least that's what my boyfriend says.' The women who were married gave similar reasons but much more influenced by the demands of domestic labour and child care.

Sandra said: 'I go to get out of the house, out from the telly and the kids and just to be able to talk to adults. I don't think to go out for a drink is the most important thing, 'cos I enjoy a drink in the house, but it's the social life.'

Jill aged fifty six, a school cleaner, with four grown-up children indicates how far attitudes towards the pub have changed, 'When I was young girls in pubs were frowned on - you daren't do it. For a long time Phil [her husband] went by 'imself with his mates, but with the children grown up, I said one day "I'm coming too". When we go I see Doris, Doris and me get along - I see her on Saturdays and have a good natter. Better than watching telly, still I don't like pubs much, never have. I go because of 'im an company. Don't go for the drink.'

The middle-class women, as in the case of Ann, had a much less routinised and regularised pattern, much more based upon what fitted in with their own pattern of behaviour shaped by non-pub relationships and choices. Some of the women went for meals, thus Liz commented: 'I often go to have a meal, sometimes I run out of vodka, so the Sucliffe is handy, also I like to take my friends there, even though the pub is "slightly up your nose", very middle class.' Jo, twenty six, a computer programmer and with a six year old son, was slightly more expansive: 'I go to the pub because it's different from home, you can talk about anything or nothing and I can get work out of my mind, I have to have somewhere to switch off from home and work. The pub is important to me also because it's neutral territory. When we have friends we can take them to the pub and stop acting hostess and they can stop behaving as guests in my house. The pub is important to me because it's the place we usually go to to have our rows - less things get broken that way.'

The reason for going to the pub seemed to overlap for the two groups of women - to get them away from the tyranny or boredom of home, kids, telly and domestic routine - and not using drinking as a reason for going to the public house. Using the pub as a neutral territory for domestic problems is itself a minor revelation but it does fit in with the anonymity and individualism of the middle-class women concerned.

One of the concerns was that of different kinds of pub, the two groups held fairly unanimous views. Joan said: 'There are different kinds of pubs- big posh ones and little scruffy ones. I prefer open ones so I can see what's going on. There are working-class pubs - at least basically. You get a few middle class dropping off at pubs but typically the working class go in their working clothes for a pint, and middle class you can tell with their suits on and have gin and tonics. '

Sandra said: 'Yes, I'd say there were. There'd be a pub we'd go in say, it's a bit rough that, 'cos you'd get fellas in their working clothes. I wouldn't go in those. Then at the other extreme there are what I would call 'posers' pubs, where you'd get these lads and they are all dressed up and you can't get to the bar for these lads in their shirts. Then there's the ones that I like, the comfortable middle pub where you get all sorts of ages, comfortable for me. I'd know the rough pub as soon as I walked in. Just by looking at it, the men in their working clothes, if there was a taproom the men would prefer it, they prefer not to go in the lounge. '

Freda when asked about different types of pubs, said: 'God, yes pubs I wouldn't go in, pubs with unshaved rough types, men who drink, God they drink. If I went in I'd want protection. Yes, rough pubs, but most are mixed, at least the one I go to is.'

Ann stated: 'In my area there is a sharp division between the pub to which I go - the Sutcliffe Arms - and the other pub which is sawdust on the floor atmosphere. It's full of cronies, people have their own seats and its all very seedy, and you get very strange looks if you go in - it's very working class. Rough pubs - all pubs are rough to me, some just have an overlay of refinement. '

Finally Lynne declares: 'The local pub is slightly up your nose, very middle class, decor isn't too posh but they try to create an impression with good food. 1 don't know about working-class pubs - where does the working class one end and the middle class one begin? I think there are rough pubs but I don't like categories, some pubs are rougher than others, depending on the state of the area in which they are based.'

What seems a conclusion offered by the women is that a gradation of pubs exist depending upon a dominant group of users - that the categories of rough, respectable, mixed and posh types have an empirical basis. We return to this in the concluding chapter.

The final question was on the picture of what happened to the pubs - what changes had occurred? Sandra said: 'I think some pubs have changed a lot, some not very much. They've modernised the lounge but people still segregate don't they, keep to their own sets.' Jo observed: 'Yes, there's an attempt to create plastic palaces"to get rid of small rooms - its too synthetic'. Lynne said: 'The divisions in pubs have been reduced, I am sure that it is good because I'm a great believer in breaking down barriers.' Jill said: 'More different people now go to pubs, they've changed in that way, less an an men's thing. A lot of pubs have been smartened up also a lot have now gone. We went to where we first married and only one of the old pubs was still left.' Finally Freda said: 'Have pubs changed? Yes they have, at least they've got more nicer to go in, not just drinking and rowdy, but some are really smart and swish.' Joan was honest if not very illuminating, '1 don't know really, they could have, I'm not sure.'

The women did suggest that there were several changes which had occurred and were occurring. The trends they thought were reasonably clear, making the pub smarter, like 'plastic palaces' , creating a 'lounge type' context, much greater range of users so that it's not just a context for men, and a reduction inthe rowdy and hard drinking element. There were some doubts expressed about such changes, people tended to 'stay in their own sets', and Jo's cryptic comments about the attempts to create 'plastic palaces' suggests that the old type of pub analysed by the Pub and the People was a recognition that separate physical spaces in the pub are useful for different groups who want to do different things, and is associated with some notion of loss of authenticity, the pub is usually becoming plastic and unauthentic.

Drinking in a Women's World

There was little evidence of women 'taking over' a pub, although 1 did find in my assessments of how women cope, evidence of opposition to the dominance of men. Pubs attempts to increase the attendance of women through 'male striptease', attempts by women to take over the pub 'for the evening' - with lesbians or women just being together as 'women', were examples of this. There is more about whether gender can take over the class basis of public house usage analysis in my final chapter.

Women were interviewed and it was discovered that none were engaged in 'pub hopping' - a feature of the working-class men. The working-class women tended to go once a week and stay for the whole evening in the pub - from 8pm until closing time. The middle-class women, as reported earlier, tended to go once a month to the pub on a much more non-pub basis, making the pub an element of personal framework of individual choice - depending on family, friends and work. They also tended to go for a shorter time period, or if they did stay going from 9pm onwards. The kinds and amount of drink consumed on a visit to the pub was remarkably similar. They all drank halves - three or four - in some cased larger, although Jill drank Velvet Stout and Sandra drank Guinness, or they drank shorts - two or three - sometimes starting with larger and finishing with a short. None of the women decided to go to a pub depending on the alcohol available. When asked why they drank, and what it did for them the women had some interesting comments.

Joan said: 'I like the feeling of being slightly drunk, I've noticed it more over the couple of months. I've been trying to lose some weight and not drink. Drink does relax me I suppose. I don't drink much during the week because of having to get up in the morning, weekends don't matter. Often I've had a drink after hours. I'd like to see pub hours extended on Friday and Saturday nights but not during the week. '

Jo said: 'Relaxation is the main effect drinking has on me. I like just to let the whole world go by, not to have things crowding in on me. It's pleasant and for me a very necessary form of relaxation. It lowers my defences I suppose and makes me more bearable to live with. I do drink more at weekends. If I had my way I'd have the pubs open all day, very much on continental lines.'

Lynne said: 'Drink for me in a pub is part of a social activity, now and again 1 go home thinking "God, that was a tough day, I could do with a drink". It makes me relax, but I don't know whether it's that one knows one has had a drink and therefore one feels one is more relaxed, and socially free, or whether its the actual drink that does it.'

Ann suggested: 'Drink, I simply drink because ifI go to a pub it seems silly to hold out against the prevailing expectation that I drink. Nothing really happens to me, I rarely have that much to drink, it doesn't make me gregarious or uninhibited, I'm pretty open as it is. I don't know whether people drink more at weekends. I've been to pubs in Ireland and seen what happens when they open all day, it doesn't matter that much to me.'

Freda said, 'I do enjoy a drink, after two or three everything seems rosier, I do get more chatty I suppose. 1 don't go for the drink but its a nice feeling. People always drink more at weekends - they've more money and time. I'd like pubs to be open all the time'.

The women did seem fairly congruent about the effects of drinking, it relaxed them everything seemed 'rosier', they could let the 'world go by' in a social world of relaxation. Some enjoyed the feeling of being slightly drunk, some the experience of dis-inhibition. The two reasons for going to the pub were the escape from work and family obligations, and joining in a time escape into relaxation with their partners, friends or known others. How far drinking had become a women's world apart from that played by men in the typical context of the pub, is an open question.

Women's Games and Entertainment

According to the women involved, their attitude to games and entertainment in pubs varied from apathy to overt hostility. Participation was almost nonexistent. The working-class women tended to be apathetic, whereas middle-class women tended to be openly hostile.

Sandra said: 'I don't play games, sometimes the jukebox, the games make no difference to me.'

Whilst Joan said: 'I don't usually play them. It doesn't appeal to me. Games are not very important at all.'

Freda said, 'I play pool sometimes but for a bit of a laugh. Games, I don't mind them if they are not too serious. I like space invaders but I'm hopeless at it.' Ann was positively hostile: 'No, I do not play pub games - those dreadful space invaders and one-armed bandits, oh Christ, they're aU irrelevant, trivial and should be banned.'

Lynne was equally hostile: 'Play games, no, it's meaningless to me, if you go to a pub you go to talk and drink. People play them because they are there _ they're not of any importance whatsoever to me.' Finally Jo said: 'I never play at the games, they wouldn't make any difference to my going to the pub. The jukebox is important - is that a game? I like background music. Frankly 1 could do without the rest. '

The women had very little interest in the games side of the public house for themselves, although they did not object to the idea of women's teams or mixed teams. They themselves however regarded the process of minimal importance in their own public house involvement.

Women and Pub Sexual Relations

I was constantly aware when talking to these women something of the possible danger of eliciting hoped-for replies. The small amount of alcohol consumed, and rejection of the games element is significant, both led to confirmation of the trust imparted. This leads to the third basis for their focal interests, their sexual and friendship patterns in the pub and a probing of their interests what they actually did in the pub. There appeared a quite remarkable similarity between the women across the pubs, so much so that one can suggest gender stratification operating in pub usage, as well as a class variable.

Joan said: 'I usually sit at a table, I wouldn't stand at the bar, though I might if I was waiting for somebody - not if! wasn't. I wouldn't go in by myself anyway.

We talk about, well, just topical things really, things that have happened during the day or anything. Joking is important - not jokes really, humour. I mean girls don't sit around telling jokes all night, I wouldn't dream of doing that. Men would. Women have a different sense of humour. At weekends (the ratio of men to women) when I see it, it's very much equal but during the week you get a few in before 8pm, middle-aged women especially. Women won't go in by themselves - it's the stigma of going in, what people would think. Men think that women by themselves are there to be picked up. They don't usually say anything to you at first. I think there's a little bit of a competition element as well, who can make the first move. It can be an embarrassment for a woman, it's enough to put me off going in a pub by myself - I wouldn't dream of doing that, not because J am afraid of what might happen, but because I would like someone to talk to and if there were only going to be men there, well, if you start talking to them, they expect to pick you up. If! saw a woman by herself I would think she was waiting for somebody, but if she was there for an hour or so, I would think she was up to something - I mean if I'm waiting for somebody I look at my watch, and turn around and look at everybody who walks through the door. People who try to pick me up - I'm usually quite nice about that, eventually they go away. Women drink as much - I mean in shorts. Women don't play many pub games - I've never heard of mixed teams, I don't think it necessary. Yes, the pub is a threatening situation for a women, generally speaking. Once a man gets a drink down him he fancies his chances, I think because I've had a few drinks as well - then one thing can lead to another. The pub is a man's world, but I'm happy as it is.'

Sandra said: 'Well, the women sit down and the men go to the bar. I wouldn't enter on my own, only to meet somebody. If I'm meeting someone, I just stand, get a drink and look very nervous until they come. If a woman walks into a pub on her own, the place goes quiet and people start to stare, so that makes you feel uncomfortable with not being used to it. If a man went by himself, they wouldn't even notice. We talk about politics, quite a lot, sex quite a lot, football sometimes, it depends, kids, but we tend not to talk about kids, we leave that alone. On Saturday night you get more women in. Women on their own though are very few. A woman on her own I'd think it was abnormal, that she was waiting for someone, but if she continued to buy drinks I don't know what I'd think. Women won't go into pubs on their own because it's a male domain. It's the attitude of the men. Perhaps them being threatened comes over. I do think you treat men differently after they've had a drink. I wouldn't argue with a man after he's had a drink, in the way that I would with a man who had not. Meself, I don't feel so much threatened, maybe it's just the unpleasantness. I don't think you can make it easier for the young girls, it's expected that a boy drinks but the girl's frowned upon. I'll never take a drink off anyone when I'm on my own. If they're talking you can just have a talk and they're pleasant, but if they start forcing themselves on you, you just have to tell them to get lost. You've got the protection of the landlord, you know, if he really starts - that's where they're different from clubs, I used to go to the club, it's just like a cattle market. The pub, a man's world? Yes, obviously if I won't go in on my own.'

Ann said: 'Don't think I've ever been to a pub by myself. I go with friends and talk. I never have any social intercourse with people I meet in the pub. What I talk about depends upon whom I'm with. One has different friends, basically current affairs, politics, the meaning of life, usually ends up with one's social and emotional problems. The ration of women to men depends on the area and the pub doesn't it? I mean the trendy pubs in town where all the eighteen year-aids collect before going to a disco, sometimes more women than men, but usually Monday to Friday mostly men, and Friday and Saturday the wives are allowed to go along. Don't think I've ever seen a woman in a pub by herself. Women don't drink as much - they usually ensconce themselves with a short and make it last. I've never seen women play games in pubs. On balance I'd say the pub is a threatening situation, men feel threatened by women coming into pubs more, and then tend to examine you minutely, and its embarrassing. You are aware that men are there in bunches, showing off slightly, a macho thing, and they make lewd remarks. Do I feel threatened by the pub - it depends on the class really, if its working-class pub and predominately young working-class, its more threatening than say a middleclass pub in Hampstead. In the north its a bit unnerving and irritating, one is constantly fighting this prejudice. It is less threatening at lunchtime and in groups, women are more protected. As a woman no, I don't think the pub would have to be invented, as a man, yes, I am sure. I don't think women have this need for reassurance, to compare notes, and outdo each other drink wise, or tale wise. Women are more self-contained, hard, they deal with their lives internally, it's hard for me to articulate. My home, my friends, I don't have a need for the pub to talk about my problems. '

Lynne expounded fully: 'I never go by myself. I take my friends with me the people I meet in the pub I regard as pains in the arse. I don't have a social life that extends around the pub. Usually I sit at a table. What one talks about depends on who one goes with, so with politically minded friends I talk politics, someone from the theatre. I have quite a wide variety of interests, I get quite political, actually, and it goes well with the pub, a political discussion. On average I would say that the ration of men to women in pubs is six to one. Women by themselves - very few. I wish I could get over my barrier and go in on my own. It's purely an upbringing thing. I would go in with another woman, right, I wouldn't go in on my own purely because you think you're being looked at. I think that women do drink as much as men, especially now, mainly in shorts. Mainly men play the games. I think that women do find the pub a threatening situation because they're going into a male environment, and you still have the sexual attitudes, women are in pubs to be picked up lots of men think that women in pubs are easy game. I have been propositioned with another girl and we just told them to "piss off". The only protection, if you are on your own, is to get up and walk out, or cause trouble - and no woman likes to do that, or very few. I have sometimes been in on my own to wait for someone, perhaps to meet someone there, I have done that, but I sit and hide because I'm on my own. It is a man's world but it doesn't have to be. It's part of social society today, that's why its a man's world. Drinking for women is something comparatively new, going out to have a drink is a breaking down of certain barriers. Certain women would still feel guilty about going to have a drink, they would be much more likely to buy a bottle in a supermarket and take it home. She doesn't have a need to go into a pub, and she doesn't have the grouping in a pub. If she's got children and wants a drink she's better off drinking at home, keeping a bottle in the fridge.'

The women all indicated that they did not go to the pub to drink per se, neither did they play the games available. They went to create and recreate in a relaxing social environment - to talk, exchange information - and yet they appeared to be very conscious of being women in a man's world. What is interesting is that all the women were aware9fthe situation, the social imagery of 'waiting for somebody', of being 'chatted up' -of being scrutinised, or mentally 'undressed' as they came into such a context was not only because the pub was used by men, it was added to by alcohol- a mild depressant which could lead to violence - they' could get ideas', and' one thing could lead to another'. The women accepted that it was a man's world, so much so that gender stereotyping was the dominant norm.

'I'd like to go by myself many a time but men who have too much drink in them can be pigs - sex mad, though after the amount some of them drink they'd be useless. I go to have a natter to the girls and relax, not to be mauled by some he-man breathing beer all over me.' (Freda)

'The way women are still not accepted as just going into a pub for a drink, makes me furious. I feel threatened if I don't have a male with me, yet it shouldn't be so. Perhaps other women don't get the looks and men approaching them - after a few drinks men will think any woman fancies them. I wish I knew how to change it, but I don't. It still makes me bloody furious.' (Jo)

What is most important is how this dislike of men, and fear of the pub where a woman could be cornered, was not age or class related, but it was sex related. As I carried out such interviews one thing became crystal clear to me, the gender basis of behaviour was possibly more important than class or age in shaping perception, or to be more precise, the criteria which applies to men, does not apply to women. The enigma unfolds as the pub provides an obvious fact. Women do not see or relate to the situation in the major free-time leisure situation in our society in the same way as men.

The Publican's Role The women were finally asked about the influence of the publican, did he make that much difference? What was the ideal landlord for these women, and what of the various aspects of his role? Two important differences emerged amongst the women: firstly the working-class customers saw the landlord as a full participant; and secondly, they were able to identify the landlord and make a clear distinction between tenants and managers.

Joan said: 'He's quite important, he should be nice and friendly with the people who are, lets face it, spending money in his pub. Friendliness, ability to mix with the regulars - especially on the pool team if they have one - and a clean pub, these are the most important things about a publican for me. The average working week depends on the size of the pub and the number of staff in a small pub just starting off I should say it's a twelve hour day. Tenants take more pride in the pub itself, managers are selective to and tend to have an arrogant attitude. Managers don't need to be as involved with the pub in the sense that it's only a firm he's working for. It doesn't matter to me whether the landlord is there or not. Running a pub? It quite appeals to me, I don't like the hours, but I think you would get compensated for that by the people. '

Sandra commented: 'If they are sort of easy going, you get that atmosphere in a pub. Yet they've got to watch it, I mean there is one local pub which shuts when he feels like it. We just won't go to that pub. The landlord - it's like an ideal host isn't it? They must not be too sociable, I mean you don't want him coming and pressing himself on you. They've got to keep a certain order but obviously they can do that in such a way as not to be dogmatic. Some you don't see behind the bar. I should think if he's behind the bar he'd probably work something like seventy hours a week. Don't think I would automatically know a managed pub - no I can't tell except at our local- mind you I'd miss her more than him when he's there. He's always among the lads. It would be the same for me if he wasn't there. Would I like the job? I wouldn't want the life - you have to be pleasant to the most unpleasant people.'

Freda said: 'He is important - you know he's going to be there and if there's aggro he'll sort it our. I like someone who's friendly and chatty - who can pass the time of day. He's got to keep a warm pub - can't abide cold pubs. What else? I like him to be part of things - to keep things going. I suppose he's got to but it's a sign of a good landlord. Work wise, well it can vary, around ten hours a day I should say. Managers do have a different way of doing things - I mean you're never sure who's in charge. If! went to a pub I didn't know I'd tell after two or three times of going. I like to know somebody's in charge but it doesn't make much difference if! know people there and I'm with people. A good pub takes a lot of doing. No, I don't think I'd run a pub 'though I'd have liked to drink the profits.'

Ann claimed: 'The publican makes a lot of difference, in the pub I go to he takes the trouble to establish one's face after three or four visits - he smiles and says hello~ how are you, gives you a warm feeling. I don't want a landlord over friendly - I don't want him knowing too much about me. I look for civility and service. He has a lot of unseen work - it can be a twelve-hour day. A good landlord? I look for friendliness, firmness, discretion - knowing when to call a halt. I wouldn't be too sure of the difference between tenants and managers - whether he's there or not I'd probably notice, but it wouldn't make much difference. Would I like to be a publican - God no!'

Lynne said in relation to the publican: 'He makes a tremendous difference it's the warmth coming from the licensee actually - sociable, and outgoing and considerate, well understanding. You can go into a pub and sometimes something upsets them, and to understand why that person has been rude, and not be rude back - which lots of publicans are. There has got to be a relationship between a publican and his customers - I think it means recognising that the person at the other side of the bar who has come in for a drink, wants something from you. It's a seven days a week contact with the public - it's a long week. Officially there is a difference between tenants and managers, for a tenant its theirs, for a manager it isn't. Logically one would expect there to be so. I've never been personally aware of the difference. It doesn't make any difference to my going to the local - he's got the staff.'

Finally Jo: 'I suppose he is important - he can be the first person one sees in a pub. He can set the tone. I want him to be pleasant, efficient but not too friendly. I don't know how long they work but longer than one would think. Managers are certainly less involved than tenants - they tend to be less sociable, more hard faced - I could give you some examples. Although I like to see the landlord I don't think he influences the pub for me. When I go to the pub I like to be with the people I'm with, if you understand my meaning. He is important but I don't like the feeling that I'm being looked at sidewise, or that I'm being chatted up by the landlord. Yes, I'd quite like to run a pub - to imprint my own personality.'

There were a number of shared elements to the discussions with these women. They all saw the manager as distinct from the tenant, having a distinct 'professional' orientation. They all wanted a friendly orientation by the landlord, but not too friendly 'pressing himself on you' , or 'knowing too much', almost as though as women they wanted to establish and maintain social distance. Almost to a woman they wanted the pub to be a public situation of private interaction. For all women the situation was different to the cultural/class variations appropriate for the men. The landlord was important to all the women, but interestingly for the 'order' element. Certainly they gave a higher rating to this than their male counterparts.

Conclusions - Women as Equal Partners

The view that women have different views from men about the pub is an established fact. The various areas looked at make a clear statement - that women have different priorities, different needs, and different interests, to those of men. Everywhere in the analysis this is the case.

Firstly women did not go to the pub to drink, or play games - 'it's the social life', as Sandra says. Alcohol relaxed them, some rather enjoyed being 'slightly drunk'. The primary focal interest was to natter, chat, gossip with their friends - to relax from the home, children, the demands of paid employment - to a focal social relationship - not to find a 'man' per se.

Secondly, it is clear that women did see very important differences between pubs - there were 'rough, respectable and posh' types - the rough type was linked to men in their 'working clothes' where they 'drank a lot', and 'women would need protection'. There was a gradation, 'where does the working-class one end and the middle-class one begin?' as Lynne said. The women interviewed did think the pubs had changed, not all for the better. Some had disappeared, some had been smartened up and become 'plastic palaces' , others had been' opened up' to create an open environment - which they liked.

Thirdly, there was an emphasis upon pub going as a weekend activity. None of the women drank a great deal in the pub, being very aware of the dangers of a 'lowering of defences', so much that she can get into 'trouble'. Things might get 'rosier' but could lead to loss of sexual control, to sexual availability. 'We are the hunters and women are the hunted', and 'any woman who comes in by herself, offers herself', were the men's comments. 'It makes me bloody furious', as Jo commented.

Fourthly, although they visited the pub, no woman would go into a pub by herself. There was something about the pub, women were 'scrutinised' or 'the place goes quiet'. She did not feel comfortable being 'sized up' by the regulars as to her availability. After all after a few drinks men 'get ideas' and think. that 'any woman fancies them'. All the women considered themselves as vulnerable, having a strong gender stereotype of what was appropriate pub behaviour.

Fifthly, the publican's role was variously important. They all wanted a sociable, friendly landlord who kept a warm, clean pub. But one who could keep control, 'who knows when to call a halt', was important. Their own participation had little to do with the publican, but when the distinction between tenants and managers was made, the managers came out as 'arrogant and hard faced', there was a difference. The picture projected by these women was for me uncomfortable. When they went to the pub one thinks they go willingly, on their own, without the fear of being assaulted, and they have aimed for some sense of equality. Perhaps this is hoped for. What is fascinating is, even in the posh pub, it is not achievable. Why not, and how far does the picture I have drawn lead to the 'sensual and masculine' culture of the pub which I have portrayed?

Chapter 11 References

I. Greer Germaine, The Whole Woman, Doubleday, 1999 pp 186-7

Chapter 12

The Public House

What we have pursued is the enigma of the pub. It is a reality which involves most of us at some level, to some degree, at some time. What has been proposed here is the microcosm of the human condition of men and women. There are various solutions to the diverse socioeconomic questions which have been raised. The distinction between rough, respectable and posh pubs has been confirmed - these are the basic types. There may be others though for the ethnic minorities - Asian, black - as well as gay and women types - there is much to be done.

There is little doubt that the pub is closely tied in with working-class culture and economic life - to judge from the historical record. There is little doubt that a considerable impact has been achieved by licensing justices who have had the effect of slowly castrating this hub of working-class culture, and with the growth of middle-class efficiency in work with the pursuit of a civilising morality. This has led to diverse consequences such as the dry, urban suburbs, the drink-drive requirements and tight egalitarian planning legislation.

These major influences have combined with the breweries concern simply to be profitable - a policy of cost-effectiveness rather than moral improvement. That the absolute decline in public houses, as well as the improvement in those that remained, is an exercise in profitability rather than a behaviour changing morality. Selling the product does not mean selling it through the public house, and the growth of' off-licence' beer and spirit sales without going through the pub, off-licence consumerism, may be a reason for this absolute decline. Especially when it followed the 'new public house' image launched after the 1947 licensing changes.

The rough, respectable and posh categories of public houses participated in, did undoubtedly appear to form a class-related continuum. Such a claim however did rest upon a male perspective and when viewed in terms of users and usage patterns, important differences emerged between the masculinity of the subculture, styles of sociability and the importance of drinking as a focal interest.

The ROUGH PUB was certainly a dominant male context. Men were rough and looked it. It was a social context in which the 'king' could take anyone out, in which there was a hierarchical ordering based on 'maleness', and one in which any woman alone who came in 'offered herself', and in which the regulars were predominantly male. It was a private context of public interaction in which sociability and drinking with mates were concreted in a sharply focused male subculture, in which bar pornography was readily available. It was a subculture reinforced by the toughness of work and unemployment, rather than predicated upon it. Women were marginal to such a world, not even joked about, regarded as 'fucking cows', but welcomed as part of the family on a Saturday night.

The RESPECTABLE PUB was very different from the rough pub. It was the first pub in which participation was attempted. What is noticeable about the process in retrospect, is that the context was the most difficult of the three public houses, yet it did yield some helpful scaffolding. It was a social context of mixed participation, a predominantly all-male bar group consisting of manual workers, a group of heterosexual predominantly manual workers, and a distinct group of non-manual or middle-class users. It was here that the different use of space was revealed, an empirical segregation of public, negotiable and private use of space existed in terms of encounters and interactions. The importance of the bar group was undoubted, it was very much like the rough pub but on a lesser scale, hard drinking in a dominant male ethos, defining women and sexuality in terms of what women were 'for', and holding the separateness as not only biological but also social in their male and female worlds. Men went to meet their 'mates', men were the 'hunters' and women the 'hunted' and regardless of age, tended to have different and distinct parallel participation modes. The mixed pub did contain non-manual workers who interacted little with others, not regarding the context as one of openness and sociability they used the pub for a private and personal interaction. They drank less in anyone period at the pub, spent comparatively less time in the pub, and their focal interest pattern was relaxation with others imported into the context - a sociability focus but very different in nature when compared to the manual workers.

The POSH PUB was distinct in its accentuation of propriety and privateness, users were predominantly white collar and professional workers and again in retrospect, when dealing with the social dynamics of the three public houses, it seemed clear that the pattern of usage and participation, was an amplification of the kinds of patterns by middle-class users of the respectable posh pub. It was the same but more so. The posh pub participants treated the pub as incidental to their own networks and friendship styles. They did not go primarily to drink, nor to play games, nor to meet 'mates' whom they usually met in the pub, they went to the public house because it offered a comfortable context of privateness. No loud music, no shouting, no men being boisterous, no fights and no loss of temper, none of the poor environment, no unpredictable landlord - none of the consequences of drunkenness - a comfortable and private context where one could chat with friends or one's partner. A context where women would feel safe - was it not only a class-based continuum but a gender-based ideology which underpinned it? The posh pub had little which was explicit in terms of a shared male subculture, little of the sex-role stereotyping process, men did take the servant role of getting drinks, but there was much evidence of women and men in the non-dichotmised social world of mutuality. Perhaps the tone was one of parallel differences which were based upon interest rather than the influence of a male-dominated culture. Was it the presence of women as equal partners, with reduction of casual violence which made the pub acceptable at one end of the spectrum? There were different kinds of pubs and there was little doubt that they did host and display distinctive views about women - masculine power based views, according to some feminists.

What, I wondered, would the feminist views be? (I) There are not other existing researches of women in pubs, none of women tenants or managers, and little except my own of how women would interact in the three types of pub. As a major institution in contemporary society the public drinking house has escaped relatively free. It is certain that pubs are class prescribed, and are they also gender prescribed? Having started with one unproven and unresearched proposition, the classification of types of pub, another has been raised from the research, how women relate to this situation. As I said little is known, apart from my research, on how women adapt and see the pub itself, whether the basis of their behaviour is gender rather than class. My feeling is that certainly it has a powerful part. Did alcohol itself have a different effect on women and men - reducing or enhancing what constitutes the sense of self? This is a question which we shall seek an answer later in this chapter.

The types of pubs seem empirically sure. The rough pub full of hard drinkers, users who were unpredictable, contexts where fists were used, women regarded as offering themselves, which hosted people 'it was not very nice to know'. Respectable pubs which hosted 'all sorts of patrons', in which women were allowed to enter, which were not just for hard drinkers and drinking, - the bar group which made itself known - but also for those seeking a quiet pint with a friend. The posh pub offered little else but a private interaction experience, no bar group, no games, no one-arm bandits, just private participation, with women treated as equal partners having a quiet chat over a drink, with no expectation of differential space usage and no expectation of deregulated behaviour.

Sex and Gender in Pubs

I have been intrigued throughout this book about the masculine subculture of the public house. Why is it that men still dominate this much beloved institution?

In answering this question one must remember that the women, by themselves, would not go into a pub. It was a threatening social context, quite simply it was a fear of being physically injured or, to a greater or lesser extent being degraded in some way. It is not easy to thread one's way through the minefield.

Firstly there are differences between the pub customers in terms of their definition of women. At the Fox and Hounds women were viewed in unambiguous terms, they were sexual objects noticeable by their absence, except prostitutes who came on Thursdays and Fridays, and wives on Saturdays, and occasional girlfriends who came with the young tough males. What is important is also complex. It was a sharply separated and distinct world. Firstly the male customer possessed a bundle of behaviours which characterised them as 'male'. There was a core matrix of masculinity to their characters. It was based on physical strength. The hierarchy had a man at the top based upon men being all powerful and successful. He was, or could be supreme. It reminded me naively of the simple fact that the pattern of conflict was hierarchical. It was almost impossible to think of it otherwise. It almost seemed a requirement to become accepted by regulars that the researcher himself was rough - to look and to listen to. There was, in other words, a shared acceptance of what was masculine - men accepted amongst themselves as physically, thus sexually and socially different from women, and separate from the world of female values and femininity. They did not see women as part of their world, they had their own world. Men saw the public house as the place where masculinity was reaffirmed, around a pint. They saw women as a part of home and family, as a woman's sexual world outside of the pub. Women were able to come for a Saturday evening when men and women were dressed up for the night out and came to the pub. It did not escape me that the men drunk not a little - on an evening they were all fairly drunk. It was a combination of physical power and hard drinking. It was this undoubted combination which enabled these men to 'feel stronger'.

Thus there is a recognition that alcohol usage by regular pub users has the effect which leads to the question, 'What does it all add up to? What have we found out in studying drinking ... Why do men drink and some to excess ... men do not drink primarily to reduce their anxiety ... as an individual alcohol, in small amounts normally consumed, has little effect on anxious thoughts although in small amounts does reduce reality ties, particularly in the form of concern about time ... nor do men drink primarily to become incompetent, to enjoy a 'time out' period in which they will be free to act without being held accountable to society for their action. There are some elements of truth in this explanation, since after drinking men feel themselves as less responsible and are less concerned about time; but it is better combined with an explanation of the positive feeling these men get from drinking. Men drink primarily to feel stronger. Those for whom personalised power is a particular concern drink more heavily. Alcohol in small amounts, in restrained social settings and in restrained people tends to increase thoughts of social power - of having an impact on others .. .in larger amounts, in impulsive settings it leads to an increase in thoughts of personalised power of winning personal victories ... in terms of sexual and aggressive conquests'. (2) What seems evident from these findings is increased drink leads to an increased sense of personal power- men as 'king', with a world 'out there', thus it all began to fall into place. The hard drinking itself reinforced the sense of physical masculinity, and this had the effect of both increased sexuality and aggressiveness. If the rough pub, and the bar group in the mixed pub, drank enough in the context of the pub, they would think they could do most things. Thus they could 'take' the woman they wanted, the world of family and work as paid employment, existed in another world -literally. The interviews carried out conflrmed such a sharp association between the normality of the rough pub, and the difficulty women experienced - difficulties not restricted to the women's use of anyone pub, but of all the pubs used. There was something about the public house as a social context in general which was simply not characteristic of the rough pub but entered into all pubs and shaped the woman '5 perceptions and experiences of the public house, irrespective of class. We will explore further this issue when we have discussed gender in the respectable and posh pubs.

The unambiguous nature of masculine subculture dominant in the rough pub was found in the working-class respectable pub. The pub bar was littered with stories about wives 'who hadn't been trained', who were' good for one thing' , and a spicy range of stories about sexual encounters and momentary conquests. It was a situation which hosted a sense of ambivalence towards women. They were nice sometimes, given men accepted their weakness and given that their soft emotional and child-centred selves was kept in check - plus their apparent willingness to involve the police. The bar group tendered to disintegrate between 8pm and l0pm when the working-class young couples came in along with occasional middle-class couples. The women who came in changed the situation but after l0pm there was a reassertion to the bar-group culture. There was involved a redefinition of sexual identities in what appears to be characteristic of middle~class ideology, if not in practice.

The posh pub had none of the overtness of sex or gender characteristic of the respectable pub. Women tended to like the Sutcliffe Arms because, 'You don't get examined as you go through the door, it's anonymous ... a nice level of conversation, I'm never going to feel uncomfortable with a fight starting'. It was a non threatening situation for the women concerned. This was the reason they went to the Sutcliffe Arms and the reason also that they would not go to a rough pub, and only go to the mixed pub with a male partner. It was a gender-based division of participation - and it was a division affecting all the women. It was based upon fear for the family, for her job, for her choice of leisure and for her friends, most of all it was fear for herself. So this pub differentiation is a story of male impropriety, of the rough context a claim for male supremacy where they exercised 'their balls not their brains', where we see a tapering down of the male demands in the respectable pub, to the flattening out of such expectations by the men in the posh pub. From 'fucking cows', to being 'chatted up' and 'needing protection', to feeling comfortable was the continuum. The woman's approach was one of adjustment to the situation, going to a pub where she 'felt comfortable'.

We live in a situation of consumer choice but if the price may be high, or the goods shoddy, or the service poor we may complain. Public openness to sociability however is part of what the pub is about, and the taming of alcohol part of what is available. Was it because the more a public house focuses around hard drinking among an all male bar group, the more likely it was that personalised power leading to sexuality and aggressive behaviour occurs? Supposing one turned this on its head, I wonder if there would be the same response in a reverse situation. It would result in the future with pubs for men and pubs for women - very boring as one woman said to me. Did such usage of alcohol by men in public result in the fear of all women - some much more than others, but all to some degree? The idea that a pub is threatening, that women would be scrutinised and chatted up, that they may be regarded as 'fucking cows', means that the threat of sexual disinhibition must be uppermost in their minds. 'Perhaps we must be clear about what being a woman involves. It means, basically being female, living in dread of annihilation or mutilation .. .let a woman protest her destiny as she may, it still remains she is female ... the point I make is that denial of the body is a delusion. No woman transcends her body'. (3) This biological reductionism one can argue with, however the threat to women in the pub remains. As has been put forward as a strong feminist argunent, 'It is virtually impossible to separate the idea of equality from the idea of similarity. If we accept that men are not free, and that masculinity is as partial an account of maleness as femininity is of femaleness, then equality must be seen to be a poor substitute for liberation. Arguing in terms of equality or difference permits two kinds of neutralising of pro-feminist pressure; one cites the concept of equality to women's disadvantage, as in the notion that women are entitled to equal work for equal pay "of equal value" - a meaningless concept that serves to enshrine women's work as permanently subordinate, the other institutionalises the contrast between men and women, treating widows differently from widowers, mothers from fathers and wives from husbands. What we find is that when it is in men's interest to plead equality, they do; when it is in their interest to plead difference, they do ... if women can see no future beyond joining the masculine elite on its own terms, our civilisation will become more destructive than ever. There has to be a better way'. (4) Is there not really a better way? Certainly there may be a situation where there is differential access, usage and consequences, as between men and women and the pub. It essentially is that women and men are different, have different needs and wants, different origins, different concerns at their different ages, have different criteria for achievement, different means by which the same problems are negotiated. The search for equality is not so much a measure by which all decisions should be judged as a basis for recognising that such differences are relevant. We are not all the same, it is a denial of individualism to suggest that we are. What is required is a measure of relevant differences. How does this situation apply to the public house, a situation where maleness and masculinity are flaunted, where femaleness and femininity are accommodated. There is growing evidence that 'relevant differences' are being accepted. It is better to watch 'vegetables growing' than see them uprooted and walls take their place.

There is another concern here, it is the implication of a 'civilising morality' for working-class culture. Such a morality may have sex and gender differences, but the evidence which has been adduced suggests that the masculine subculture of the public house, may be a major limit on the role of 'civilising morality' equated with a middle-class view of industrial society. The public house is a resilient, flexible and changing institution, it has many faults, but it is a persistent focus of working-class leisure. What seems to have happened is that the middle class, with their own definitions and limitations, have become absorbed in it. It is in a real sense pre-industrial, a coalescence of experience and values, retaining an elemental and naturalistic male/female dichotomy, overlaid by the industrial division of labour and in conflict with an economising efficiency characteristic of industrial capitalism and post-industrial society. As yet the conflict between women and the public house is yet to be researched and resolved.

The Publican and Women

Have we lost the publican in the debate about sex, class and the pub? Not intentionally. Historically each of them has performed a secretive and influential part of what has been provided by the brewing companies. In the existing situation all three pubs in the observation and interviewing process had tenants, yet each displayed a part over which the brewer had little control- what the breweries called the 'social side' of the pub. Each publican played a part in the way women related to the men involved in drinking at the pub and at being a regular there.

The rough pub was keyed completely into the publican's role. He was very much part of the masculine subculture, hard talking, hard drinking, as the regulars said "im's one of us' . What he did prohibit was minimal. There was a constant conflict with his family over the pub, and he was never behind the bar. The respectable pub was not dissimilar so far as the women were concerned where the publican was a participant, playing pool, drinking with the lads and a member of the hard-drinking bar group. He was at the centre of the masculine subculture, it was him who insulated the male regulars from the wives who phoned, he who facilitated a constant flow of jokes and comments about women in particular. He was also central in the information and black market network, almost anything could be negotiated for in the pub. The penetration of the work side of the pub totally invaded the family, so much so it drove his wife 'bloody barmy'. Life for her was one of constant crisis management, trying to keep a home together, looking after 'kids' and serving in the pub. His view about women was fairly unequivocal, they were 'the hunted'. As far as he was concerned they had to earn their place at his bar and 'adjust' to his views about women in the pub.

The posh pub was different. The publican was not known for drinking at the bar, was not one of the regulars, was not involved with the games or pool area. He kept separate his personal views about women, which were crude sexist jokes to several repartee. He lived next to the pub, therefore there was no overspill from the pub to the family. He exercised the norms of privateness and propriety - and there was a mutuality in terms of heterosexual relationships. The interesting thing about the publican's attitude was the sharp distinction he made between family life and pub life. Women were regarded as important as men - not by the publican, but he recognised that this is what his customers preferred.

The Public Drinking House

The phenomenon we have explored is a difficult subject. The individual customers have had little indication of just how difficult. The present state of knowledge leads us to certain conclusions. These empirically-grounded propositions are the bases for existing and future research, as well as where we are at the present time.

I. The public drinking house has been historically ubiquitous. It has been an important nexus of working-class culture and social life, containing existing class differences in lifestyles and values and forms ofleisure which both reflect and perpetuate class differences.

2. The effects of post-war brewery and licensing - planning policies have

revealed the mixing of the different categories of usage, increasingly the likelihood of social and economic stratification between public houses, and fostering changes in the focal interests of the participants.

3. The existing public drinking house is socially stratified in terms of contexts on a class basis - with rough, respectable and posh public houses forming elements on an empirical continuum of socioeconomic differentiation, fostering and nurturing different categories of users and usages.

4. Important differences between public houses are revealed in the usage patterns which are class and sex related. The focal interests of users constitute leisure and gender salience hierarchies, such hierarchies importantly coalesce around the nature of sociability, the nature of sex and gender, and the importance attached to drinking in the pub.

5. Male working-class public house regulars use the public house as a private situation of public interaction - it is a social context relationally separate from family and work, where situational interaction with mates is shared, and where relationships are renewed in face-to-face encounters in an activity-oriented masculine subculture, in which hard drinking is an important element.

6. Middle-class users of the pub regarded it as a public situation of private interaction - it is a situation which is relationally continuous with family and work, a place to bring friends and partners for face-to-face encounters, but in an anonymous and interpersonal world of passivity and sexual mutuality, and where alcohol usage is an incidental social lubricant rather than an important element in the social matrix.

7. For all male users of the public house the time was one of relaxation and a pleasurable experience, as a social context with minimal obligation and constraint, enabling maximum choice over their modes of participation, but each class differing fundamentally in their sociability styles and the meaning of using the pub.

8. Women regulars of the pub tended to display similar class differences of sociability styles and usage patterns of male users, however such similarities are shaped by a sexual dimension which structures usage and participation. The pub is viewed as a masculine context in which women may be defined as sexually available, in which the men may elementally view women in biological sexual terms. Men perceive women in sexual terms and this is accentuated by the consumption of alcohol which reduces the norms which may regulate gender relationships and behaviour.

9. The difference in class and gender usage of the pub influences and are influenced by, the work style of the publican. The more the publican integrates the family and leisure with work, the greater the incorporation of his lifestyle

into the lifestyles and values of the dominant group of users. The more working class the dominant group of users, in terms of open sociability, the greater the interdependence of time, relational and activity dimensions in the symbiosis of the life of the publican.

10. Women appear, regardless of class, to use the public house in a different way to that of men. The men sought women on a sexual basis overtly whilst the women were inclined on a sexual basis to judge the relationship. Women were fearful of the consequences of excess alcohol consumption. More research is required as to why women think and feel vulnerable.

These propositions are not intended as other than empirically derived conclusions grounded in the study undertaken. The public drinking house does seem to be class-based leisure. There does appear an umbilical link for men between the position in the division of labour, the values of masculinity, and usage of the public house. Such a finding may say much about a context of unparalleled flexibility and cultural centrality for those who have nothing to lose but their labour power. Those who espouse the public house as a way of life, do so in which song, sin and sensuality are an essentially appealing to human communality and human freedom. Those for whom a civilising morality and rational recreation appears to mean a denial of the essential self and akin to a routinised and unnatural mode of being. A study of the public drinking house appears to be nothing less than a study of the loss of community consequent upon the division of labour, the growth of individualism and rationalism, the emergence of a highly segmented work, family and gender structure, and profound adherence to a context which, in its various forms, encapsuJates a microcosm of social reality.

In a year when we look backwards, to a chequered history, and forward to a brighter and gender-influenced but not determined future, the penultimate word perhaps deservedJy is contained in the Mass

Observation study of 1942. 'The pub is still very much a pre-industrial institution .. a sort of bridge between the older institutions and those new ones catering for people strictly as individuals ... human societies have only been maintained by limitation on their member's freedom by restrictions ... between man and man. The internal stability of a society is dependent upon the general observance of these things. They have become natural constrain, and modify instinctive urges. One of the features that differentiates our "civilised" society most clearly is the weakening of these forms of restrictions ... but while these restrictions have weakened another type has become very strong, those imposed by the actual economic structure of society'. (5)

We are at a new beginning. If women can detach themselves from the cluster of emotional elements which compose their self identity, and if men can accept this different if equal status, we may have moved the goal posts of the public drinking house. We have opened Pandora's box and unleashed the four horsemen of class, gender, leisure and alcohol. IfI have kept you to this point in seeking to explain this enigma, you have a set of empirically-grounded propositions and a basis on which to proceed. Much is yet to be explained and understood, particularly within a framework which seeks a generous definition of human behaviour. Knowledge should be cumulative if never final. The social life of the pub - its prognosis, problems and solutions - must be analysed in the gender-based industrial society geared into the new century. Women and men in relation to this enigma, without losing their sense of dignity and identity, should learn that equality does not mean losing the difference which makes the pub a worthwhile institution in this new millennium.

Chapter 12 References

1.   The story is told of the difficulty for the overtly radical feminist, who could not cope with the decor of Tommy Ducks, a well-known Manchester pub, what was the action they resorted to? They pulled down the knickers and bras which hung from the ceiling, and sprayed pictures of the topless barmaids with paint. The publican was quite philosophical about the scene, he said the women's clothing needed washing and customers wouldn't come if they did not like the atmosphere - after all the underclothes were donated by the patrons themselves.

2.   McClelland D.C., The Drinking Man, The Free Press, New York, 1972, pp332-335

3.   Rheingold J.C., The Fear of Being a Woman, Grune and Stratton, New York,1964,p2l5

4.   Greer, Gennaine, The Whole Woman, Doubleday- Transworld, London, 1999, p308-309

5.   Gollancz, Victor, The Pub and the People, Mass Observation, London, 1943

www.ingramcontent.com/pod-product-compliance
Lightning Source LLC
Chambersburg PA
CBHW080044280326
41935CB00014B/1781

* 9 7 8 1 9 0 8 9 0 4 2 9 4 *